NOSTALGIA FOR D

&

HIEROGLYPHS OF DESIRE

Nostalgia for Death

POETRY BY

XAVIER VILLAURRUTIA

TRANSLATED BY ELIOT WEINBERGER

&

Hieroglyphs of Desire

A CRITICAL STUDY OF VILLAURRUTIA BY

OCTAVIO PAZ

TRANSLATED BY ESTHER ALLEN

———

EDITED BY ELIOT WEINBERGER

———

COPPER CANYON PRESS

Publication of this book is supported by a grant from
the Fideicomiso para la Cultura México-Estados Unidos
and a grant from the National Endowment for the Arts.
Additional support to Copper Canyon Press has been
provided by the Andrew W. Mellon Foundation,
the Lannan Foundation, the Lila Wallace-Reader's Digest Fund,
and the Washington State Arts Commission.
Copper Canyon Press is in residence with Centrum
at Fort Worden State Park.

COPPER CANYON PRESS
Post Office Box 271
Port Townsend, Washington 98368
THIRD PRINTING
Library of Congress Cataloging-in-Publication Data
Villaurrutia, Xavier, 1904–1950.
[Nostalgia de la muerte. English]
Nostalgia for death : poetry / by Xavier Villaurrutia ; translated
by Eliot Weinberger. With Villaurrutia : hieroglyphs of desire : an
essay on the poetry / by Octavio Paz ; translated by Esther Allen.
p.   cm.
ISBN 1-55659-053-9 : $12.00
1. Villaurrutia, Xavier, 1904–1950–Criticism and interpretation.
I. Paz, Octavio, 1914–   Villaurrutia. English. 1992. II. Title.
III. Title: Villaurrutia.
PQ7297.V6N5813   1992
861–dc20   92-17926

CONTENTS

Editor's note / 1

Nostalgia de la muerte / Nostalgia for Death
TRANSLATED BY ELIOT WEINBERGER

NOCTURNOS / NOCTURNES
Nocturno / Nocturne / 5
Nocturno miedo / Nocturne: Fear / 9
Nocturno grito / Nocturne: The Scream / 11
Nocturno de las estatua / Nocturne: The Statue / 13
Nocturno en que nada se oye / Nocturne: Nothing Is Heard / 15
Nocturno sueño / Nocturne: Dream / 19
Nocturno preso / Nocturne: Imprisoned / 23
Nocturno amor / Nocturne: Love / 25
Nocturno solo / Nocturne: Alone / 29
Nocturno eterno / Nocturne: The Eternal / 31
Nocturno muerto / Nocturne: The Dead / 35

OTROS NOCTURNOS / OTHER NOCTURNES
Nocturno / Nocturne / 37
Nocturno en que habla la muerte / Nocturne: Death Speaks / 41
Nocturno de los ángeles / L.A. Nocturne: The Angels / 44
Nocturna rosa / Nocturne: The Rose / 51
Nocturno mar / Nocturne: The Sea / 55
Nocturno de la alcoba / Nocturne: The Bedroom / 59
Cuando la tarde . . . / When Evening . . . / 63
Estancias nocturnas / Nocturnal Stanzas / 65

NOSTALGIAS

Nostalgia de la nieve / Nostalgia for Snow / 67

Cementerio en la nieve / Cemetery in the Snow / 69

North Carolina Blues / 71

Muerte en el frío / Death in the Cold / 75

Paradoja del miedo / The Paradox of Fear / 79

Volver . . . / To Go Back . . . / 83

Décima muerte / Death in Décimas / 85

Hieroglyphs of Desire

TRANSLATED BY ESTHER ALLEN

Xavier with an X / 95

Things Seen and Unforeseen / 113

The Sleeper Awake / 125

EDITOR'S NOTE

MY TRANSLATION of Xavier Villaurrutia's poems began in early 1990 as a direct response to what I was reading in the newspapers. Though soon to be diverted by another foreign war, American patriots at the time were enraged by the specter of "federally financed pornography." This meant artworks, not to the taste of certain religious groups and politicians, whose makers or exhibitors had received grants from the National Endowment for the Arts. Two museums had their funds cut, two artists and one museum director were arrested as pornographers, and various forms of self-censorship multiplied in sectors of the arts dependent on such support. All recipients of NEA money had to sign a statement – written by the conservative ideologue Jesse Helms and passed by a cowardly Senate – that they would not "promote, disseminate or produce obscene or indecent materials," which were defined, among other things, as "including but not limited to depictions of sadomasochism, homoeroticism, the exploitation of children, or individuals engaged in sex acts."

Though the whole business was ludicrous – producing panic in the arts without the slightest effect in the pornography industry – it was particularly disturbing to have national legislation that equated any form of homoeroticism with sociopathic activity. Beyond the obvious psychological refutations, and the catalog of master artists and writers who were or are homosexual, it seemed to me evident that the universality of any erotic art is based on the irrelevancy of its object of affection. The erotic poem – to speak only of poetry – occurs only in the past or in the future; it is memory or it is desire. It is an act of imagination that speaks to another imagination, which in turn will translate it into its own memories and desires. The human body is abstract in a poem; what is tangible – there for our senses – is the body of the poem.

Xavier Villaurrutia (1903–1950) was homosexual, and one of the only writers in Latin America in the first half of the century who was openly gay. He was a major poet who wrote essentially one book of poetry – *Nostalgia for Death* (1938, expanded 1946), presented here in its entirety – and a scattering of other poems. Yet his influence, particularly on the succeeding generation of Octavio Paz and others, has been enormous. Technically, he took the prosody and many of the themes of Spanish *modernismo* (our Symbolism) and stripped its high-flown rhetoric to the natural, condensed and playful speech of the Spanish *vanguardia* (our Modernism). But most of all, he was one of the great poets of desire: one whose beloved, finally, is not another man but Death itself, Death himself. He could hardly have foreseen that time would turn some of these poems into bitter, eerie prophecies of individual lives in an epidemic.

He is a poet I've thought of translating for years. What sent me to work on these poems was the belief that, beyond all the letters and petitions, all of us in a Helms America – regardless of our tastes and practices in private life, and regardless of what we normally write – had a duty to produce more such "pornography," to expose the absurdity with further concrete examples, and – with a little nostalgia for the days of the avant-garde – to work in such a way that no one would give us money for it.

– E W

NOSTALGIA FOR DEATH

(NOSTALGIA DE LA

MUERTE)

Xavier Villaurrutia

TRANSLATED BY ELIOT WEINBERGER

Burned in a sea of ice, and drowned amidst a fire.

— MICHAEL DRAYTON

NOCTURNO

Todo lo que la noche
dibuja con su mano
de sombra:
el placer que revela,
el vicio que desnuda.

Todo lo que la sombra
hace oír con el duro
golpe de su silencio:
las voces imprevistas
que a intervalos enciende,
el grito de la sangre,
el rumor de unos pasos
perdidos.

Todo lo que el silencio
hace huir de las cosas:
el vaho del deseo,
el sudor de la tierra,
la fragancia sin nombre
de la piel.

Todo lo que el deseo
unta en mis labios:
la dulzura soñada
de un contacto,
el sabido sabor
de la saliva.

Y todo lo que el sueño
hace palpable:
la boca de una herida,
la forma de una entraña,

NOCTURNE

Everything the night sketches
with its shadowy hand:
the pleasures it reveals,
the vices it undresses.

Everything the shadows
make you hear
in the hard thudding silence:
the sudden voices
that randomly flare,
the bloody scream,
the rustle of a few lost
steps.

Everything the silence
makes things emit:
the haze of desire,
the sweat of earth,
the unlabeled perfume
of the skin.

Everything that desire
smudges across my lips:
the sweet dream
of contact,
the salient savor
of saliva.

And everything that sleep
makes you touch:
the mouth of a wound,
the shape of a gut,

la fiebre de una mano
que se atreve.

¡Todo!
circula en cada rama
del árbol de mis venas,
acaricia mis muslos,
inunda mis oídos,
vive en mis ojos muertos,
muere en mis labios duros.

the heat of a hand
that dares reach over.

Everything
circulates through every branch
of the tree of my veins.
It caresses my thighs,
it pushes my head under,
it lives in my deadening eyes,
and dies on my hardening lips.

NOCTURNO MIEDO

Todo en la noche vive una duda secreta:
el silencio y el ruido, el tiempo y el lugar.
Inmóviles dormidos o despiertos sonámbulos
nada podemos contra la secreta ansiedad.

Y no basta cerrar los ojos en la sombra
ni hundirlos en el sueño para ya no mirar,
porque en la dura sombra y en la gruta del sueño
la misma luz nocturna nos vuelve a desvelar.

Entonces, con el paso de un dormido despierto,
sin rumbo y sin objeto nos echamos a andar.
La noche vierte sobre nosotros su misterio,
y algo nos dice que morir es despertar.

¿Y quién entre las sombras de una calle desierta,
en el muro, lívido espejo de soledad,
no se ha visto pasar o venir a su encuentro
y no ha sentido miedo, angustia, duda mortal?

El miedo de no ser sino un cuerpo vacío
que alguien, yo mismo o cualquier otro, puede ocupar,
y la angustia de verse fuera de sí, viviendo,
y la duda de ser o no ser realidad.

NOCTURNE: FEAR

Everything lives at night in secret doubt:
silence and sound, place and time.
Asleep unmoving or sleepwalking awake,
nothing can be done for that secret dread.

And it's useless to close your eyes in the shadows,
to sink them in sleep so they'll not keep seeing,
for in the hardening shadows, the cave of dreams,
the same nocturnal light will wake you again.

Then, with the shuffle of the suddenly woken,
aimlessly, pointlessly, you start walking.
Night spills its mysteries over you,
and something tells you that to die is to wake up.

In the shadows of a deserted street, on a wall,
in the deep purple mirror of loneliness, who
hasn't seen himself on the way to or from some
     encounter,
and not felt the fear and wretchedness and fatal doubt?

The fear of being nothing but an empty body
that anybody – I or anyone else – could occupy,
and the wretchedness of watching yourself, alive,
and the doubt that it is – it is not – real.

Tengo miedo de mi voz
y busco mi sombra en vano.

¿Será mía aquella sombra
sin cuerpo que va pasando?
¿Y mía la voz perdida
que va la calle incendiando?

¿Qué voz, qué sombra, qué sueño
despierto que no he soñado
serán la voz y la sombra
y el sueño que me han robado?

Para oír brotar la sangre
de mi corazón cerrado,
¿pondré la oreja en mi pecho
como en el pulso la mano?

Mi pecho estará vacío
y yo descorazonado
y serán mis manos duros
pulsos de mármol helado.

NOCTURNE: THE SCREAM

I'm afraid of my own voice.
Uselessly I search for my shadow.

That shadow with no body
passing by – is that one mine?
Or that voice, lost,
wandering the streets setting fires?

What voice, what shadow, what waking
dream I've yet to dream
could be the voice, the shadow,
the dream they've stolen from me?

To hear the blood burst
from my sealed heart,
will I put my ear to my chest
like fingers on a pulse?

My chest will be empty
and I disheartened
and my hands hard pulses
of chilly marble.

NOCTURNO DE LA ESTATUA

a Agustín Lazo

Soñar, soñar la noche, la calle, la escalera
y el grito de la estatua desdoblando la esquina.

Correr hacia la estatua y encontrar sólo el grito,
querer tocar el grito y sólo hallar el eco,
querer asir el eco y encontrar sólo el muro
y correr hacia el muro y tocar un espejo.
Hallar en el espejo la estatua asesinada,
sacarla de la sangre de su sombra,
vestirla en un cerrar de ojos,
acariciarla como a una hermana imprevista
y jugar con las fichas de sus dedos
y contar a su oreja cien veces cien cien veces
hasta oírla decir: "estoy muerta de sueño."

NOCTURNE: THE STATUE

for Agustín Lazo

Dream, dream of night, the street, the stairway
and the scream of the statue unrounding the corner.

Run to the statue, and find only the scream,
long to touch the scream, and find only its echo,
long to grasp the echo, and find only the wall,
run to the wall and touch a mirror.
Find in the mirror the assassinated statue,
pull it out from the blood of its shadow,
dress it in a flutter of eyes,
caress it like a sister who suddenly appears,
shuffle the chips of its fingers
and repeat in its ear a hundred times a hundred
      hundred times
until you hear it say: "I'm dying of sleep."

En medio de un silencio desierto como la calle antes del crimen
sin respirar siquiera para que nada turbe mi muerte
en esta soledad sin paredes
al tiempo que huyeron los ángulos
en la tumba del lecho dejo mi estatua sin sangre
para salir en un momento tan lento
en un interminable descenso
sin brazos que tender
sin dedos para alcanzar la escala que cae de un piano invisible
sin más que una mirada y una voz
que no recuerdan haber salido de ojos y labios
¿qué son labios? ¿qué son miradas que son labios?
y mi voz ya no es mía
dentro del agua que no moja
dentro del aire de vidrio
dentro del fuego lívido que corta como el grito
Y en el juego angustioso de un espejo frente a otro
cae mi voz
y mi voz que madura
y mi voz quemadura
y mi bosque madura
y mi voz quema dura
como el hielo de vidrio
como el grito de hielo
aquí en el caracol de la oreja
el latido de un mar en el que no sé nada
en el que no se nada
porque he dejado pies y brazos en la orilla

NOCTURNE: NOTHING IS HEARD

In the middle of a silence deserted as a street before a crime
not even breathing so that nothing will disturb my dying
in this loneliness with no walls
at this hour when angles are escaping
I leave my bloodless statue in the tomb of my bed
and go off in the slow-moving moment
in the interminable descent
with no arms to stretch out
with no fingers to reach the scale falling from an invisible piano
with nothing more than a glance and a voice
that can't remember having left their eyes and lips
what are lips? what are glances that are lips?
and my voice is no longer my voice
within this unwetting water
within this plate glass air
within this purple fire that slashes like a scream
In the miserable game of mirror to mirror
my voice is falling
and my voice incinerates
and my voice in sin narrates
and my voice in sin elates
and my poison scintillates
like plate glass ice
like the screams of ice
here in the shell of my ear
the pounding of a sea where I get nothing
wet nothing
for I've left my arms and feet on shore

siento caer fuera de mí la red de mis nervios
mas huye todo como el pez que se da cuenta
hasta ciento en el pulso de mis sienes
muda telegrafía a la que nadie responde
porque el sueño y la muerte nada tienen ya que decirse.

and I feel the net of my nerves being cast outside me
and everything escapes like a calculating fish
counting to a hundred in the pulse in my temples
a dead telegraph no one is answering
for sleep and death have nothing more to say.

NOCTURNO SUEÑO

a Jules Supervielle

Abría las salas
profundas el sueño
y voces delgadas
corrientes de aire
entraban

Del barco del cielo
del papel pautado
caía la escala
por donde mi cuerpo
bajaba

El cielo en el suelo
como en un espejo
la calle azogada
dobló mis palabras

Me robó mi sombra
la sombra cerrada
Quieto de silencio
oí que mis pasos
pasaban

El frío de acero
a mi mano ciega
armó con su daga
Para darme muerte
la muerte esperaba

Y al doblar la esquina
un segundo largo
mi mano acerada
encontró mi espalda

NOCTURNE: DREAM

for Jules Supervielle

Sleep was unfolding
its measureless swings
and thin voices
currents of air
drifted in

Down the rungs
of the musical score
of the ship of the sky
my body
descended

The sky on the ground
like a mirror
The silvered street
bent my words

Thickening shadows
stole my shadow
Silent in the silence
I heard my steps
go by

The chill of steel
on my groping hand
armed me with its dagger
Death waited
to bring me death

And around the corner
a long second later
my steeled hand found
my back

Sin gota de sangre
sin ruido ni peso
a mis pies clavados
vino a dar mi cuerpo

Lo tomé en los brazos
lo llevé a mi lecho

Cerraba las alas
profundas el sueño

Without a drop of blood
soundless weightless
my body came
on nailed feet

I took it in my arms
I carried it to my bed

Sleep was folding
its measureless wings

Prisionero de mi frente
el sueño quiere escapar
y fuera de mí probar
a todos que es inocente.
Oigo su voz impaciente,
miro su gesto y su estado
amenazador, airado.
No sabe que soy el sueño
de otro: si fuera su dueño
ya lo habría libertado.

NOCTURNE: IMPRISONED

Held prisoner in my mind
the dream wants to escape
and prove its innocence
to everyone on the outside.
I hear its impatient voice,
see its gestures, its furious
menacing state.
It doesn't know that I'm the dream
of another: that if I were its keeper
I'd have set it free.

NOCTURNO AMOR

a Manuel Rodríquez Lozano

El que nada se oye en esta alberca de sombra
no sé cómo mis brazos no se hieren
en tu respiración sigo la angustia del crimen
y caes en la red que tiende el sueño
Guardas el nombre de tu cómplice en los ojos
pero encuentro tus párpados más duros que el silencio
y antes que compartirlo matarías el goce
de entregarte en el sueño con los ojos cerrados
sufro al sentir la dicha con que tu cuerpo busca
el cuerpo que te vence más que el sueño
y comparo la fiebre de tus manos
con mis manos de hielo
y el temblor de tus sienes con mi pulso perdido
y el yeso de mis muslos con la piel de los tuyos
que la sombra corroe con su lepra incurable
Ya sé cuál es el sexo de tu boca
y lo que guarda la avaricia de tu axila
y maldigo el rumor que inunda el laberinto de tu oreja
sobre la almohada de espuma
sobre la dura página de nieve
No la sangre que huyó de mí como del arco huye la flecha
sino la cólera circula por mis arterias
amarilla de incendio en mitad de la noche
y todas las palabras en la prisión de la boca
y una sed que en el agua del espejo
sacia su sed con una sed idéntica
De qué noche despierto a esta desnuda
noche larga y cruel noche que ya no es noche
junto a tu cuerpo más muerto que muerto
que no es tu cuerpo ya sino su hueco
porque la ausencia de tu sueño ha matado a la muerte
y es tan grande mi frío que con un calor nuevo

NOCTURNE: LOVE

for Manuel Rodríguez Lozano

Nothing is heard hearing himself swimming in this pool of shadows
I don't know how my arms aren't bruised by your breathing
as I follow in the wretchedness of crime
and you fall into the net that's stretched by sleep
In your eyes you hold the name of your accomplice
but your eyelids are harder than silence
and you'd rather kill than share that joy of sinking
eyes closed into sleep
I suffer from the pleasure with which your body searches
for a body to conquer you more than sleep
comparing the heat of your hands
with my icy hands
the quivering of your temples with my faint pulse
the plaster cast of my thighs with the skin of your thighs
that the shadows are corroding with incurable leprosy
Now I know what the sex of your mouth is
what the greed of your armpit holds close
and I curse the whispers that have flooded the labyrinth of your ear
on the breakers of the pillow
on the hard page of snow
Not the blood shot from me like an arrow from a bow
but the rage circling through my veins
flaming yellow in the middle of the night
and all the words in the prison of my mouth
the thirst which in the mirror's water
slakes its thirst with another identical thirst
From what night do I wake to this undressed night
long cruel night now no longer night
next to your body more dead than dead
that is not your body but the impression of your body
for the absence of your dream has murdered death
and my coldness is so vast that with a new heat

abre mis ojos donde la sombra es más dura
y más clara y más luz que la luz misma
y resucita en mí lo que no ha sido
y es un dolor inesperado y aún más frío y más fuego
no ser sino la estatua que despierta
en la alcoba de un mundo en el que todo ha muerto.

it opens my eyes where the shadow is hardest
and clearest and more light than light itself
and it resurrects in me what has never been
and it is a sudden pain even colder more fiery
to be nothing but the statue that wakes
in the bedroom of a world where everything is dead.

Soledad, aburrimiento,
vano silencio profundo,
líquida sombra en que me hundo,
vacío del pensamiento.
Y ni siquiera el acento
de una voz indefinible
que llegue hasta el imposible
rincón de un mar infinito
a iluminar con su grito
este naufragio invisible.

NOCTURNE: ALONE

Loneliness, boredom,
useless bottomless silence,
I'm sunk in liquid shadows,
all thought blanked out.
And not even the inflection
of an indefinable voice
to reach the impossible corner
of an infinite sea
to illuminate screaming
this invisible wrecked ship.

Cuando los hombres alzan los hombros y pasan
o cuando dejan caer sus nombres
hasta que la sombra se asombra

cuando un polvo más fino aún que el humo
se adhiere a los cristales de la voz
y a la piel de los rostros y las cosas

cuando los ojos cierran sus ventanas
al rayo del sol pródigo y prefieren
la ceguera al perdón y el silencio al sollozo

cuando la vida o lo que así llamamos inútilmente
y que no llega sino con un nombre innombrable
se desnuda para saltar al lecho
y ahogarse en el alcohol o quemarse en la nieve

cuando la vi cuando la vid cuando la vida
quiere entregarse cobardemente y a oscuras
sin decirnos siquiera el precio de su nombre

cuando en la soledad de un cielo muerto
brillan unas estrellas olvidadas
y es tan grande el silencio del silencio
que de pronto quisiéramos que hablara

o cuando de una boca que no existe
sale un grito inaudito
que nos echa a la cara su luz viva
y se apaga y nos deja una ciega sordera

NOCTURNE: THE ETERNAL

When men straighten their shoulders and go by
when they let their names drop away
till even the shadows show shock

when a dust finer than smoke
clings to the crystals of a voice
and the skin of faces and the skin of things

when eyes shut their windows
to the rays of the prodigal sun, preferring
blindness to forgiveness, silence to sobbing

when life or what we uselessly call life
when it arrives with its unnameable name
undresses to leap into bed
and drown in alcohol or burn in snow

when I when if when lie when life
wants to meekly surrender in the dark
without even naming the price of its name

when a few forgotten stars still shine
in the loneliness of the dead sky
and the silence of silence is so vast
we wish it could speak

or when a mouth that does not exist
screams an inaudible scream
that showers our faces with living light
then flickers out, leaving us deaf and blind

o cuando todo ha muerto
tan dura y lentamente que da miedo
alzar la voz y preguntar "quién vive"

dudo si responder
a la muda pregunta con un grito
por temor de saber que ya no existo

porque acaso la voz tampoco vive
sino como un recuerdo en la garganta
y no es la noche sino la ceguera
lo que llena de sombra nuestros ojos

y porque acaso el grito es la presencia
de una palabra antigua
opaca y muda que de pronto grita

porque vida silencio piel y boca
y soledad recuerdo cielo y humo
nada son sino sombras de palabras
que nos salen al paso de la noche

or when everything has died
so hard so slow we're terrified
to raise our voices and ask "who's left?"

and I doubt I should answer
that unspoken question with a scream
for fear of discovering I no longer exist

for perhaps my voice too is no longer alive
except as a memory in my throat
and it is not the night but blindness
that fills our eyes with shadows

for perhaps the scream is the presence
of an ancient word
an opaque speechless word that suddenly screams

for life silence skin and mouth
solitude memory sky and smoke
are nothing but the shadows of words
to hold back, for us, the night

NOCTURNO MUERTO

Primero un aire tibio y lento que me ciña
como la venda al brazo enfermo de un enfermo
y que me invada luego como el silencio frío
al cuerpo desvalido y muerto de algún muerto.

Después un ruido sordo, azul y numeroso,
preso en el caracol de mi oreja dormida
y mi voz que se ahogue en ese mar de miedo
cada vez más delgada y más enardecida.

¿Quién medirá el espacio, quién me dirá el momento
en que se funda el hielo de mi cuerpo y consuma
el corazón inmóvil como la llama fría?

La tierra hecha impalpable silencioso silencio,
la soledad opaca y la sombra ceniza
caerán sobre mis ojos y afrentarán mi frente.

NOCTURNE: THE DEAD

First the slow and tepid air will tighten round me
like a bandage on the infected arm of an infected man
and invade me like the cold silence
of some dead man's dead homeless body.

Then the blue, soundless, countless racket
jailed in the sleeping shell of my ear
as my voice drowns in that sea of fear
growing weaker, growing more inflamed.

Who can stake out the space, foretell the moment
when the ice will overrun my body and envelop
this unpulsing heart like a cold flame?

Earth turned to untouchable silent silence,
lightless loneliness and ashen shadow
will fall over my eyes, will deface my face.

NOCTURNO

Al fin llegó la noche con sus largos silencios,
con las húmedas sombras que todo lo amortiguan.
El más ligero ruido crece de pronto y, luego,
muere sin agonía.

El oído se aguza para ensartar un eco
lejano, o el rumor de unas voces que dejan,
al pasar, una huella de vocales perdidas.

¡Al fin llegó la noche tendiendo cenicientas
alfombras, apagando luces, ventanas últimas!

Porque el silencio alarga lentas manos de sombra.
La sombra es silenciosa, tanto que no sabemos
dónde empieza o acaba, ni si empieza o acaba.

Y es inútil que encienda a mi lado una lámpara:
la luz hace más honda la mina del silencio
y por ella desciendo, inmóvil, de mí mismo.

Al fin llegó la noche a despertar palabras
ajenas, desusadas, propias, desvanecidas:
tinieblas, corazón, misterio, plenilunio...

¡Al fin llegó la noche, la soledad, la espera!

Porque la noche es siempre el mar de un sueño antiguo,
de un sueño hueco y frío en el que ya no queda
del mar sino los restos de un naufragio de olvidos.

Porque la noche arrastra en su baja marea
memorias angustiosas, temores congelados,

NOCTURNE

In the end night fell with its long silences,
with its damp shadows that muffle everything.
A thin sound suddenly swells, then
painlessly dies.

The ear sharpens to thread a far-off echo,
or the murmur of a few passing voices
that leave behind a trail of vowels.

In the end night fell unrolling ash-strewn carpets,
putting out the lights, shutting the last windows.

For silence stretches out its slow shadowy hands,
and the shadow is silent, so silent we never know
where it begins or ends, if it begins or ends.

And it's useless to switch on the lamp at my side,
for light only makes the mineshaft of silence deeper
as I descend, unmoving, from my self.

In the end night fell to wake other people's
words, old-fashioned, proper, yellowed words:
darkness, heart, mystery, harvest moon . . .

In the end night, loneliness, hope fell!

For the night is always the sea of an ancient dream,
a cold empty dream in which nothing of the sea is left
but the debris of a shipwreck of oblivion.

For the night's low tide drags
painful memories, icy fears,

la sed de algo que, trémulos, apuramos un día,
y la amargura de lo que ya no recordamos.

¡Al fin llegó la noche a inundar mis oídos
con una silenciosa marea inesperada,
a poner en mis ojos unos párpados muertos,
a dejar en mis manos un mensaje vacío!

the thirst for something that, trembling, we finish off
    one day,
and the bitterness of what we no longer remember.

In the end night falls to push my head under
its silent unexpected tide,
to cover my eyes with dead eyelids
and leave a blank message in my hands.

NOCTURNO EN QUE HABLA
LA MUERTE

Si la muerte hubiera venido aquí, a New Haven,
escondida en un hueco de mi ropa en la maleta,
en el bolsillo de uno de mis trajes,
entre las páginas de un libro
como la señal que ya no me recuerda nada;
si mi muerte particular estuviera esperando
una fecha, un instante que sólo ella conoce
para decirme: "Aquí estoy.
Te he seguido como la sombra
que no es posible dejar así nomás en casa;
como un poco de aire cálido e invisible
mezclado al aire duro y frío que respiras;
como el recuerdo de lo que más quieres;
como el olvido, sí, como el olvido
que has dejado caer sobre las cosas
que no quisieras recordar ahora.
Y es inútil que vuelvas la cabeza en mi busca:
estoy tan cerca que no puedes verme,
estoy fuera de ti y a un tiempo dentro.
Nada es el mar que como un dios quisiste
poner entre los dos;
nada es la tierra que los hombres miden
y por la que matan y mueren;
ni el sueño en que quisieras creer que vives
sin mí, cuando yo misma lo dibujo y lo borro;
ni los días que cuentas
una vez y otra vez a todas horas,
ni las horas que matas con orgullo
sin pensar que renacen fuera de ti.
Nada son estas cosas ni los innumerables
lazos que me tendiste,
ni las infantiles argucias con que has querido dejarme

NOCTURNE: DEATH SPEAKS

If death had come here, to New Haven,
hidden in the folds of the clothes in my suitcase,
in the pocket of one of my suits,
in the pages of a book
like a note that reminds me of nothing;
if my own death were waiting for a day,
a moment known only to itself
to say: "Here I am.
I've been following you like the shadow
that can't be left at home,
like a bit of warm invisible air
mixed with the hard cold air you breathe;
like the memory of that which you love most;
like oblivion, yes like the oblivion
you've let fall over the things
you no longer want to remember.
It's useless to turn your head away:
I'm so close you can't see me,
I'm outside you and within.
Nothing is the sea that, like a god, you wanted
to put between us;
nothing is the earth that men stake out
and for which they kill and die;
nor the dream in which you want to believe that
    you're alive
without me, when I myself sketch and erase it;
nor the days that you count,
one after another, at all hours;
nor the hours you kill with pride
without thinking that they'll be reborn without you.
These things are nothing, like the countless
traps you set for me,
like the childish sophistries with which you tried

engañada, olvidada.
Aquí estoy, ¿no me sientes?
Abre los ojos; ciérralos, si quieres."

Y me pregunto ahora,
si nadie entró en la pieza contigua,
¿quién cerró cautelosamente la puerta?
¿Qué misteriosa fuerza de gravedad
hizo caer la hoja de papel que estaba en la mesa?
¿Por qué se instala aquí, de pronto, y sin que yo la invite,
la voz de una mujer que habla en la calle?

Y al oprimir la pluma,
algo como la sangre late y circula en ella,
y siento que las letras desiguales
que escribo ahora,
más pequeñas, más trémulas, más débiles,
ya no son de mi mano solamente.

to trick me, forget me.
Here I am, can't you feel me?
Open your eyes; or close them if you prefer."

And now I ask myself,
if no one entered the next room,
who so carefully closed the door?
What mysterious force of gravity
made that sheet of paper fall from the table?
Why is there suddenly, uninvited,
the voice of a woman talking in the street?

And pressing down my pen,
something like blood pulses and circulates inside it,
and I know that the crooked letters
I now write,
tinier, shakier, more faint,
no longer come from my hand alone.

NOCTURNO DE LOS ANGELES

a Agustín J. Fink

Se diría que las calles fluyen dulcemente en la noche.
Las luces no son tan vivas que logren desvelar el secreto,
el secreto que los hombres que van y vienen conocen,
porque todos están en el secreto
y nada se ganaría con partirlo en mil pedazos
si, por el contrario, es tan dulce guardarlo
y compartirlo sólo con la persona elegida.

Si cada uno dijera en un momento dado,
en sólo una palabra, lo que piensa,
las cinco letras del DESEO formarían una enorme cicatriz luminosa,
una constelación más antigua, más viva aún que las otras.
Y esa constelación sería como un ardiente sexo
en el profundo cuerpo de la noche,
o, mejor, como los Gemelos que por vez primera en la vida
se miraran de frente, a los ojos, y se abrazaran ya para siempre.

De pronto el río de la calle se puebla de sedientos seres,
caminan, se detienen, prosiguen.
Cambian miradas, atreven sonrisas,
forman imprevistas parejas...

Hay recodos y bancos de sombra,
orillas de indefinibles formas profundas
y súbitos huecos de luz que ciega
y puertas que ceden a la presión más leve.

El río de la calle queda desierto un instante.
Luego parece remontar de sí mismo
deseoso de volver a empezar.
Queda un momento paralizado, mudo, anhelante
como el corazón entre dos espasmos.

L.A. NOCTURNE: THE ANGELS

for Agustín J. Fink

You might say the streets flow sweetly through the night.
The lights are dim so the secret will be kept,
the secret known by the men who come and go,
for they're all in on the secret
and why break it up in a thousand pieces
when it's so sweet to hold it close,
and share it only with the one chosen person.

If, at a given moment, everyone would say
with one word what he is thinking,
the six letters of DESIRE would form an enormous luminous scar,
a constellation more ancient, more dazzling than any other.
And that constellation would be like a burning sex
in the deep body of night,
like the Gemini, for the first time in their lives,
looking each other in the eyes and embracing forever.

Suddenly the river of the street is filled with thirsty creatures;
they walk, they pause, they move on.
They exchange glances, they dare to smile,
they form unpredictable couples . . .

There are nooks and benches in the shadows,
riverbanks of dense indefinable shapes,
sudden empty spaces of blinding light
and doors that open at the slightest touch.

For a moment, the river of the street is deserted.
Then it seems to replenish itself,
eager to start again.
It is a paralyzed, mute, gasping moment,
like a heart between two spasms.

Pero una nueva pulsación, un nuevo latido
arroja al río de la calle nuevos sedientos seres.
Se cruzan, se entrecruzan y suben.
Vuelan a ras de tierra.
Nadan de pie, tan milagrosamente
que nadie se atrevería a decir que no caminan.

¡Son los ángeles!
Han bajado a la tierra
por invisibles escalas.
Vienen del mar, que es el espejo del cielo,
en barcos de humo y sombra,
a fundirse y confundirse con los mortales,
a rendir sus frentes en los muslos de las mujeres,
a dejar que otras manos palpen sus cuerpos febrilmente,
y que otro cuerpos busquen los suyos hasta encontrarlos
como se encuentran al cerrarse los labios de una misma boca,
a fatigar su boca tanto tiempo inactiva,
a poner en libertad sus lenguas de fuego,
a decir las canciones, los juramentos, las malas palabras
en que los hombres concentran el antiguo misterio
de la carne, la sangre y el deseo.

Tienen nombres supuestos, divinamente sencillos.
Se llaman Dick o John, o Marvin o Louis.
En nada sino en la belleza se distinguen de los mortales.
Caminan, se detienen, prosiguen.
Cambian miradas, atreven sonrisas.
Forman imprevistas parejas.

Sonríen maliciosamente al subir en los ascensores de los hoteles
donde aún se practica el vuelo lento y vertical.
En sus cuerpos desnudos hay huellas celestiales;

But a new throbbing, a new pulsebeat
launches new thirsty creatures on the river of the street.
They cross, crisscross, fly up.
They glide along the ground.
They swim standing up, so miraculously
no one would ever say they're not really walking.

They are angels.
They have come down to earth
on invisible ladders.
They come from the sea that is the mirror of the sky
on ships of smoke and shadow,
they come to fuse and be confused with men,
to surrender their foreheads to the thighs of women,
to let other hands anxiously touch their bodies
and let other bodies search for their bodies till they're found,
like the closing lips of a single mouth,
they come to exhaust their mouths, so long inactive,
to set free their tongues of fire,
to sing the songs, to swear, to say all the bad words
in which men have concentrated the ancient mysteries
of flesh, blood and desire.

They have assumed names that are divinely simple.
They call themselves *Dick* or *John*, *Marvin* or *Louis*.
Only by their beauty are they distinguishable from men.
They walk, they pause, they move on.
They exchange glances, they dare to smile.
They form unpredictable couples.

They smile maliciously going up in the elevators of hotels,
where leisurely vertical flight is still practiced.
There are celestial marks on their naked bodies:

signos, estrellas y letras azules.
Se dejan caer en la camas, se hunden en las almohadas
que los hacen pensar todavía un momento en las nubes.
Pero cierran los ojos para entregarse mejor a los goces de su
    encarnación misteriosa,
y, cuando duermen, sueñan no con los ángeles sino con los mortales.

blue signs, blue stars and letters.
They let themselves fall into beds, they sink into pillows
that make them think they're still in the clouds.
But they close their eyes to surrender to the pleasures of their
      mysterious incarnation,
and when they sleep, they dream not of angels but of men.

NOCTURNO ROSA

a José Gorostiza

Yo también hablo de la rosa.
Pero mi rosa no es la rosa fría
ni la de piel de niño,
ni la rosa que gira
tan lentamente que su movimiento
es una misteriosa forma de la quietud.

No es la rosa sedienta,
ni la sangrante llaga,
ni la rosa coronada de espinas,
ni la rosa de la resurrrección.

No es la rosa de pétalos desnudos,
ni la rosa encerada,
ni la llama de seda,
ni tampoco la rosa llamarada.

No es la rosa veleta,
ni la úlcera secreta,
ni la rosa puntual que da la hora,
ni la brújula rosa marinera.

No, no es la rosa rosa
sino la rosa increada,
la sumergida rosa,
la nocturna,
la rosa inmaterial,
la rosa hueca.

Es la rosa del tacto en las tinieblas,
es la rosa que avanza enardecida,
la rosa de rosadas uñas,

NOCTURNE: THE ROSE

for José Gorostiza

I too speak of the rose.
But my rose is not a cold rose
or the rose of a boy's skin,
or the rose that turns
so slowly its motion
is a mysterious form of stillness.

It is not the thirsty rose,
or the bleeding wound,
or the crown of thorns,
or the rose of the resurrection.

It is not the rose of naked petals,
or the wax rose,
or the flame of silk,
or the flaming rose.

It is not the weathervane rose,
or the secret rot,
or the punctual rose that rings the hour,
or the rose marine compass.

No, it's not the rose rose,
but the uncreated rose,
the sunken rose,
the nocturnal,
immaterial rose,
the empty rose.

It is the rose of touching in darkness,
the rose aroused,
the rose of rosy fingernails,

la rosa yema de los dedos ávidos,
la rosa digital,
la rosa ciega.

Es la rosa moldura del oído,
la rosa oreja,
la espiral del ruido,
la rosa concha siempre abandonada
en la más alta espuma de la almohada.

Es la rosa encarnada de la boca,
la rosa que habla despierta
como si estuviera dormida.
Es la rosa entreabierta
de la que mana sombra,
la rosa entraña
que se pliega y expande
evocada, invocada, abocada,
es la rosa labial,
la rosa herida.

Es la rosa que abre los párpados,
la rosa vigilante, desvelada,
la rosa del insomnio desojada.

Es la rosa del humo,
la rosa de ceniza,
la negra rosa de carbón diamante
que silenciosa horada las tinieblas
y no ocupa lugar en el espacio.

the fingertip rose of avid hands,
the digital rose,
the blind rose.

It is the rose mold of the ear,
the rose of hearing,
the spiral of sound,
the conch shell rose that is always abandoned
on the highest wave of the pillow.

It is the incarnate rose of the mouth,
the rose awake that speaks
as though it were asleep.
It is the half-open rose
from which the shadows rise,
the rose of entrails
that unfold and expand,
evoked, invoked, unyoked,
it is the labial rose,
the wounded rose.

It is the rose that opens its eyes,
the sleepless rose, watching over,
the rose of straining insomniac eyes.

It is the rose of smoke,
the rose of ash,
the black rose of the carbon diamond
that silently drills through the darkness
and takes up no room in space.

NOCTURNO MAR

a Salvador Novo

Ni tu silencio duro cristal de dura roca,
ni el frío de la mano que me tiendes,
ni tus palabras secas, sin tiempo ni color,
ni mi nombre, ni siquiera mi nombre
que dictas como cifra desnuda de sentido;

ni la herida profunda, ni la sangre
que mana de sus labios, palpitante,
ni la distancia cada vez más fría
sábana nieve de hospital invierno
tendida entre los dos como la duda;

nada, nada podrá ser más amargo
que el mar que llevo dentro, solo y ciego,
el mar antiguo edipo que me recorre a tientas
desde todos los siglos,
cuando mi sangre aún no era mi sangre,
cuando mi piel crecía en la piel de otro cuerpo,
cuando alguien respiraba por mí que aún no nacía.

El mar que sube mudo hasta mis labios,
el mar que se satura
con el mortal veneno que no mata
pues prolonga la vida y duele más que el dolor.
El mar que hace un trabajo lento y lento
forjando en la caverna de mi pecho
el puño airado de mi corazón.

Mar sin viento ni cielo,
sin olas, desolado,
nocturno mar sin espuma en los labios,
nocturno mar sin cólera, conforme
con lamer las paredes que lo mantienen preso

NOCTURNE: THE SEA

for Salvador Novo

Not your hard rock-crystal hard silence,
not the cold of the hand you extend me,
not your sapless, seasonless, colorless words,
not my name, not even my name,
which you pronounce as a blank and meaningless cipher;

not the deep gash, not the blood
dripping from your quivering lips,
not the distance, each time a little colder,
a sheet of snow in the hospital of winter,
stretching between us like doubt;

nothing, nothing could be more bitter
than the sea I carry inside me, blind, alone,
the ancient Oedipal sea randomly washing over me
from all the centuries, from the ages
when my blood wasn't yet my blood,
when my skin grew on the skin of another body,
when someone was breathing for the unborn me.

The sea that rises speechless to my lips,
the sea satiated
with a fatal poison that doesn't kill,
that prolongs life, and is more painful than pain.
The sea that does its work slowly and slowly
in the cavern of my chest forging
the angry fist of my heart.

Windless, skyless sea,
waveless, desolate,
nocturnal breakerless sea at my lips,
nocturnal angerless sea, content
to lap the walls that hold it prisoner,

y esclavo que no rompe sus riberas
y ciego que no busca la luz que le robaron
y amante que no quiere sino su desamor.

Mar que arrastra despojos silenciosos,
olvidos olvidados y deseos,
sílabas de recuerdos y rencores,
ahogados sueños de recién nacidos,
perfiles y perfumes mutilados,
fibras de luz y náufragos cabellos.

Nocturno mar amargo
que circula en estrechos corredores
de corales arterias y raíces
y venas y medusas capilares.

Mar que teje en la sombra su tejido flotante,
con azules agujas ensartadas
con hilos nervios y tensos cordones.

Nocturno mar amargo
que humedece mi lengua con su lenta saliva,
que hace crecer mis uñas con la fuerza
de su marea oscura.

Mi oreja sigue su rumor secreto,
oigo crecer sus rocas y sus plantas
que alargan más y más sus labios dedos.

Lo llevo en mí como un remordimiento,
pecado ajeno y sueño misterioso,
y lo arrullo y lo duermo
y lo escondo y lo cuido y le guardo el secreto.

slave that never breaks out of its shore,
blindman that never looks for the light they stole from it,
lover that craves only disaffection.

Sea that drags its silent junk,
desires, derelict derelictions,
syllables from memories and ill will,
the drowned dreams of newborn babies,
the mutilated silhouettes and perfumes,
the strands of light and shipwrecked hair.

Nocturnal bitter sea
that circulates through the narrow corridors
of coral veins and roots
and arteries and capillary jellyfish.

Sea weaving its drifting weaving in the shadows,
threading its blue needles
with threads of nerves and tendons taut.

Nocturnal bitter sea
that wets my tongue with its lugubrious saliva,
that makes my fingernails grow
with the force of its dark tides.

My ear follows its secret babble,
and I hear it growing the rocks and plants
that extend its fingers and lips.

And I carry it inside me like regret,
like someone else's sin, a mysterious dream,
and I rock it and put it to sleep,
and hide it, take care of it, a secret I keep.

La muerte toma siempre la forma de la alcoba
que nos contiene.

Es cóncava y oscura y tibia y silenciosa,
se pliega en las cortinas en que anida la sombra,
es dura en el espejo y tensa y congelada,
profunda en las almohadas y, en las sábanas, blanca.

Los dos sabemos que la muerte toma
la forma de la alcoba, y que en la alcoba
es el espacio frío que levanta
entre los dos un muro, un cristal, un silencio.

Entonces sólo yo sé que la muerte
es el hueco que dejas en el lecho
cuando de pronto y sin razón alguna
te incorporas o te pones de pie.

Y es el ruido de hojas calcinadas
que hacen tus pies desnudos al hundirse en la
      alfombra.

Y es el sudor que moja nuestros muslos
que se abrazan y luchan y que, luego, se rinden.

Y es la frase que dejas caer, interrumpida.
Y la pregunta mía que no oyes,
que no comprendes o que no respondes.

Y el silencio que cae y te sepulta
cuando velo tu sueño y lo interrogo.

NOCTURNE: THE BEDROOM

Death always takes the shape
of our bedroom.

It is concave and dark, silent and warm,
it gathers in the curtains where the shadows take
     shelter,
it is hard in the mirror and icy and tense,
deep in the pillows, white in the sheets.

We both know that death takes the shape
of our bedroom, and that in our bedroom
there's a cold space that erects
a wall, a crystal, a silence between us.

Then, only I know that death
is the hollow you leave in our bed
when suddenly, for no reason,
you sit up, or you stand.

And it is the crackling of burning leaves
your bare feet make across the rug.

And it is the sweat that wets our thighs
that lock and struggle and then surrender.

And it is the sentence you interrupt and let drop.
And my question you don't hear,
you don't understand, you don't answer.

And the silence that falls and entombs you
as I watch over your sleep and wonder.

Y solo, sólo yo sé que la muerte
es tu palabra trunca, tus gemidos ajenos
y tus involuntarios movimientos oscuros
cuando en el sueño luchas con el ángel del sueño.

La muerte es todo esto y más que nos circunda,
y nos une y separa alternativamente,
que nos deja confusos, atónitos, suspensos,
con una herida que no mana sangre.

Entonces, sólo entonces, los dos solos, sabemos
que no el amor sino la oscura muerte
nos precipita a vernos cara a cara a los ojos,
y a unirnos y a estrecharnos, más que solos y
      náufragos,
todavía más, y cada vez más, todavía.

And I, only I, know that death
is the choked words, the strange groans
and the obscure involuntary movements you make
when you wrestle the angel of sleep in your sleep.

Death is all this and more that encircles us,
and brings us together, pulls us apart,
and finally leaves us confused, startled, hanging,
with a wound that doesn't bleed.

Then, only then, both of us alone know
that it is not love, but darkening death
that makes us look, face and face in each other's eyes,
and reach and come together, more than alone and
            stranded,
still more, and each time more, even still.

Cuando la tarde cierra sus ventanas remotas,
sus puertas invisibles,
para que el polvo, el humo, la ceniza,
impalpables, oscuros,
lentos como el trabajo de la muerte
en la cuerpo del niño,
vayan creciendo;
cuando la tarde, al fin, ha recogido
el último destello de luz, la última nube,
el reflejo olvidado y el ruido interrumpido,
la noche surge silenciosamente
de ranuras secretas,
de rincones ocultos,
de bocas entreabiertas,
de ojos insomnes.

La noche surge con el humo denso
del cigarrillo y de la chimenea.
La noche surge envuelta en su manto de polvo.
El polvo asciende, lento.
Y de un cielo impasible,
cada vez más cercano y más compacto,
llueve ceniza.

Cuando la noche de humo, de polvo y de ceniza
envuelve la ciudad, los hombres quedan
suspensos un instante,
porque ha nacido en ellos, con la noche, el deseo.

WHEN EVENING...

When evening shuts its distant windows
and invisible doors,
so that dust, smoke, ashes,
impalpable, dark,
slow as the work of death
in a boy's body,
start to grow;
when evening, at last, has gathered
the last glint of light, the last cloud,
the abandoned reflection, the interrupted sound,
the night then silently surges
from secret furrows,
from hidden corners,
from half-open mouths,
from insomniac eyes.

Night surges with the dense smoke
of cigarettes and chimneys.
Night surges wrapped in its cape of dust.
The dust slowly rises,
and out of an impenetrable sky,
growing closer, denser,
ashes rain.

When smoky dusty ashen night
wraps around the city, men hold back,
suspended for a moment,
for at night, born within them, is desire.

Sonámbulo, dormido y despierto a la vez,
en silencio recorro la ciudad sumergida.
¡Y dudo! Y no me atrevo a preguntarme si es
el despertar de un sueño o es un sueño mi vida.

En la noche resuena, como en un mundo hueco,
el ruido de mis pasos prolongados, distantes.
Siento miedo de que no sea sino el eco
de otros pasos ajenos, que pasaron mucho antes.

Miedo de no ser nada más que un jirón del sueño
de alguien – ¿de Dios? – que sueña en este mundo amargo.
Miedo de que despierte ese alguien – ¿Dios? –, el dueño
de un sueño cada vez más profundo y más largo.

Estrella que te asomas, temblorosa y despierta,
tímida aparción en el cielo impasible,
tú, como yo – hace siglos –, estás helada y muerta,
mas por tu propia luz sigues siendo visible.

¡Seré polvo en el polvo y olvido en el olvido!
Pero alguien, en la angustia de una noche vacía,
sin saberlo él, ni yo, alguien que no ha nacido
dirá con mis palabras su nocturna agonía.

NOCTURNAL STANZAS

Sleepwalking, both asleep and awake,
I silently cross the sunken city.
And I doubt! And I dare not ask
if my life is a dream, or from a dream awaking.

At night, as though the world were hollow,
the sound of my footsteps, far off, protracted.
And I fear they're nothing but the echoes
of someone else's steps that passed here long ago.

The fear of being nothing more than a scrap of the dream
of someone – is it God? – who dreams in this bitter world.
The fear that this someone – is it God? – master
of a lengthening, deepening sleep, will wake.

Star, you appear awake and quivering,
shy apparition in the impenetrable sky,
you, like me, for centuries have been cold and dead,
but by your own light you still are visible.

I will be dust in the dust, oblivion's oblivion,
but someone in the wretchedness of some empty night,
without his knowing, without my knowing, someone still unborn
will with my words speak the sorrows of his night.

¡Cae la noche sobre la nieve!

Todos hemos pensado alguna vez
o alguien – yo mismo – lo piensa ahora
por quienes no saben que un día lo pensaron ya,
que las sombras que forman la noche de todos los días
caen silenciosas, furtivas, escondiéndose
detrás de sí mismas, del cielo:
copos de sombra.
Porque la sombra es la nieve oscura,
la impensable callada nieve negra.

¡Cae la nieve sobre la noche!

¡Qué luz de atardecer increíble,
hecha del polvo más fino,
llena de misteriosa tibieza,
anuncia la aparición de la nieve!
Luego, por hilos invisibles
y sueltos en el aire como una cabellera,
descienden
copos de pluma, copos de espuma.

Y algo de dulce sueño,
de sueño sin angustia,
infantil, tierno, leve
goce no recordado
tiene la milagrosa
forma en que por la noche
caen las silenciosas
sombras blancas de nieve.

NOSTALGIA FOR SNOW

Night falls on the snow!

We have all at one time thought,
or someone – I myself – am thinking it now
for those who don't know they once thought it,
that the shadows that form the night every day,
silently, furtively, hiding themselves
behind themselves, fall from the sky:
snowflakes of shadows.
For shadows are dark snow,
the unimaginable black still snow.

Snow falls on the night!

What light of incredible evening,
composed of the finest dust,
full of mysterious slight warmth,
announces the apparition of snow.
Then, on invisible threads,
loose in the air like unpinned hair,
the white-capped flakes and flakes of down
come down.

And something from a sweet dream,
from an untroubled dream,
childish, tender, a fragile
unremembered joy
takes on the miraculous form
of night and its falling, silent,
white shadows of snow.

A nada puede compararse un cementerio en la nieve.
¿Qué nombre dar a la blancura sobre lo blanco?
El cielo ha dejado caer insensibles piedras de nieve
sobre las tumbas,
y ya no queda sino la nieve sobre la nieve
como la mano sobre sí misma eternamente posada.

Los pájaros prefieren atravesar el cielo,
herir los invisibles corredores del aire
para dejar sola la nieve,
que es como dejarla intacta,
que es como dejarla nieve.

Porque no basta decir que un cementerio en la nieve
es como un sueño sin sueños
ni como unos ojos en blanco.

Si algo tiene de un cuerpo insensible y dormido,
de la caída de un silencio sobre otro
y de la blanca persistencia del olvido,
¡a nada puede compararse un cementerio en la nieve!

Porque la nieve es sobre todo silenciosa,
más silenciosa aún sobre las losas exangües:
labios que ya no pueden decir una palabra.

CEMETERY IN THE SNOW

Nothing can compare with a cemetery in the snow.
What name could be given to this whiteness on white?
The sky has dropped insensible stones
of snow on the tombs,
and nothing is left but snow on snow
like a hand forever poised over itself.

Birds prefer, crossing the sky,
to gouge invisible corridors of air,
and to leave the snow alone,
leaving it intact,
leaving it snow.

For it's not enough to say that a cemetery in the snow
is like sleep without dreams,
or eyes gone blank.

For something with an insensible, sleeping body,
with the fall of one silence over another
and the white persistence of oblivion,
nothing can compare with a cemetery in the snow!

For snow is, above all, silent,
and more silent still on the bloodless graves:
lips that can no longer say a word.

NORTH CAROLINA BLUES

a Langston Hughes

En North Carolina
el aire nocturno
es de piel humana.
Cuando lo acaricio
me deja, de pronto,
en los dedos,
el sudor de una gota de agua.

En North Carolina

Meciendo el tronco vertical,
desde las plantas de los pies
hasta las palmas de las manos
el hombre es árbol otra vez.

En North Carolina

Si el negro ríe,
enseña granadas encías
y frutas nevadas.
Mas si el negro calla,
su boca es una roja
entraña.

En North Carolina

¿Cómo decir
que la cara de un negro se ensombrece?

En North Carolina

Habla un negro:
— Nadie me entendería

NORTH CAROLINA BLUES

for Langston Hughes

In North Carolina
the night air
is made of human skin.
Caressing it,
it leaves
a drop of sweat
on my fingers.

In North Carolina

Trunk swaying,
branches of veins
in the palm of a hand,
man is a tree again.

In North Carolina

Pomegranate gums
and snow-white fruit
when a black man laughs.
But if he is silent,
his mouth is a red
gizzard.

In North Carolina

How does one say
a black man's face grew dark?

In North Carolina

A black man speaks:
"No one would understand me

si dijera que hay sombras blancas
en pleno dia.

En North Carolina

En diversas salas de espera
aguardan la misma muerte
los pasajeros de color
y los blancos, de primera.

En North Carolina

Nocturnos hoteles:
llegan parejas invisibles,
las escaleras suben solas,
fluyen los corredores,
retroceden las puertas,
cierran los ojos las ventanas.
Una mano sin cuerpo
escribe y borra negros
nombres en la pizarra.

En North Carolina

Confundidos
cuerpos y labios,
yo no me atrevería
a decir en la sombra:
Esta boca es la mía.

En North Carolina

if I said there are white shadows
in the middle of the day."

In North Carolina

In two waiting rooms
they await the same death:
the colored passengers
and the whites in first class.

In North Carolina

Nocturnal hotel:
the invisible couples arrive,
the stairs separately climbing,
the hallways rushing down,
the doors retreating behind,
the eyes of the windows closing.
A disembodied hand
writes and erases
black names on the blackboard.

In North Carolina

Tangled
lips and bodies,
and I in the shadows
would never dare to say:
This mouth is mine.

In North Carolina

MUERTE EN EL FRIO

Cuando he perdido toda fe en el milagro,
cuando ya la esperanza dejó caer la última nota
y resuena un silencio sin fin, cóncavo y duro;

cuando el cielo de invierno no es más que la ceniza
de algo que ardió hace muchos, muchos siglos;

cuando me encuentro tan solo, tan solo,
que me busco en mi cuarto
como se busca, a veces, un objeto perdido,
una carta estrujada, en los rincones;

cuando cierro los ojos pensando inútilmente
que así estaré más lejos
de aquí, de mí, de todo
aquello que me acusa de no ser más que un muerto,

siento que estoy en el infierno frío,
en el invierno eterno
que congela la sangre en las arterias,
que seca las palabras amarillas,
que paraliza el sueño,
que pone una mordaza de hielo a nuestra boca
y dibuja las cosas con una línea dura.

Siento que estoy viviendo aquí mi muerte,
mi sola muerte presente,
mi muerte que no puedo compartir ni llorar,
mi muerte de que no me consolaré jamás.

Y comprendo de una vez para nunca
el clima del silencio

DEATH IN THE COLD

When I have lost all faith in miracles,
when hope has dropped its final note
and is echoed by an endless, hard and concave silence;

when the winter sky is nothing more than the ashes
of something burnt many many centuries ago;

when I find myself alone, so alone,
that I look for myself in my room
the way one looks for some misplaced thing,
a crumpled letter in some corner;

when I close my eyes to uselessly imagine
that I'm far away
from here, from me, from everything
that accuses me of being nothing but a corpse,

then I feel I'm in cold winter,
in the eternal winter
that freezes the blood in my veins,
that chaps the yellow words,
that paralyzes dreams,
that puts a muzzle of ice on our mouths
and sketches things with a hard line.

I feel that here I'm living my death,
my solitary present death,
my death I can't share, can't mourn,
my death for which I'll never be consoled.

And I know, for once and forever,
the climate of silence

donde se nutre y perfecciona la muerte.
Y también la eficacia del frío
que preserva y purifica sin consumir como el fuego.

Y en el silencio escucho dentro de mí el trabajo
de un minucioso ejército de obreros que golpean
con diminutos martillos mi linfa y mi carne estremecidas;

siento cómo se besan
y juntan para siempre sus orillas
las islas que flotaban en mi cuerpo;

cómo el agua y la sangre
son otra vez la misma agua marina,
y cómo se hiela primero
y luego se vuelve cristal

y luego duro mármol,
hasta inmovilizarme en el tiempo más angustioso y lento,
con la vida secreta, muda e imperceptible
del mineral, del tronco, de la estatua.

in which death feeds and becomes perfect.
And the efficacy of the cold
that preserves and purifies, without consuming like a flame.

And in the silence I hear within me the work
of an army of miniscule workers pounding
with tiny hammers my lymph glands and shaken flesh;

I feel how they kiss one another,
attaching forever the shores
of the islands that float in my body;

how water and blood
are once again the same sea-water,
how first they freeze,
then turn to glass,
and then hard marble
till I'm immobilized in a slower, more wretched, time
with the secret, speechless, imperceptible life
of a rock, a tree trunk, a statue.

PARADOJA DEL MIEDO

¡Cómo pensar, un instante siquiera,
que el hombre mortal vive!
El hombre está muerto de miedo,
de miedo mortal a la muerte.

El miedo lo acompaña como la sombra al cuerpo.
le asalta en las tinieblas,
se revela en su sueño,
toma, a veces, la forma del valor.

Y sin embargo existe un miedo, miedo mayor,
mayor aún que el miedo a la muerte,
un miedo más miedo aún:
el miedo a la locura,
el miedo indescriptible
que dura la eternidad del espasmo
y que produce el mismo doloroso placer;
el miedo de dejar de ser uno mismo
ya para siempre,
ahogándose en un mundo
en que ya las palabras y los actos
no tengan el sentido que acostumbramos darles;
en un mundo en que nadie,
ni nosotros mismos,
podamos reconocernos:
"¿Éste soy yo?"
"¡Éste no, no eres tú!"

O el miedo de llegar a ser uno mismo
tan directa y profundamente
que ni los años, ni la consunción ni la lepra,
nada ni nadie
nos distraiga un instante

THE PARADOX OF FEAR

To think, if only for a moment,
that mortal man is actually alive!
Man has dropped dead from fear,
from the mortal fear of death.

Death follows him like a body's shadow,
it assaults him in the dark,
reveals itself in his dreams,
takes, at times, the form of courage.

And yet there is a fear, a great fear,
greater than the fear of death,
a fear more fear than fear:
the fear of madness,
the indescribable fear
that lasts the eternity of a spasm
and that creates the same painful pleasure;
the fear of no longer being yourself
forever,
sunk in a world where acts and words
have other meanings;
in a world where no one,
not even ourselves
can recognize us:
"Is this me?"
"No, that's not you!"

Or the fear of becoming one's self
so clearly, so profoundly,
that neither years nor consumption nor leprosy,
nothing and no one
can distract us for a moment

de nuestra perfecta atención a nosotros mismos,
haciéndonos sentir nuestra creciente,
irreversible parálisis.

¡Cuántas veces nos hemos sorprendido exclamando
desde el más recóndito pozo de nuestro ser
y por boca de nuestras heridas extrañas:
"¡Pero si no estoy loco!"
"¡Acaso crees que estoy muerto!"

Y no obstante ese miedo,
ese miedo mortal a la muerte,
lo hemos sentido todos,
una vez y otra vez,
atrayente como el vacío,
como el peligro, como el roce
que va derecho al espasmo,
al espasmo que es la sola muerte
que la bestia y el hombre conocen y persiguen.

¿Y qué vida sería la de un hombre
que no hubiera sentido, por una vez siquiera,
la sensación precisa de la muerte,
y luego su recuerdo,
y luego su nostalgia?

Si la sustancia durable del hombre
no es otra sino el miedo;
y si la vida es un inaplazable
mortal miedo a la muerte,
puesto que ya no puede sentir miedo,
puesto que ya no puede morir,
sólo un muerto, profunda y valerosamente,
puede disponerse a vivir.

from the total attention to ourselves
that makes us feel our growing,
irreversible paralysis.

How many times have we surprised ourselves claiming
from the most hidden well of our being
through the mouth of our strange wounds:
"But I'm not crazy!"
"You must think I'm dead!"

And yet there is that fear,
that mortal fear of death
we've all felt
now and again,
fascinating as the void,
as danger, as the friction
that leads directly to the spasm,
the spasm that is the only death
that beast and man know and seek out.

What would be the life of a man
who had never felt, not even once,
the precise sensation of death,
and then its memory,
and then the nostalgia for it?

If the enduring stuff of man
is nothing else but fear;
if life is an inescapable
mortal fear of death,
given that he can no longer feel fear,
given that he can no longer die,
only a dead man, profoundly and courageously,
can prepare himself for life.

VOLVER...

Volver a una patria lejana,
volver a una patria olvidada,
oscuramente deformada
por el destierro en esta tierra.
¡Salir del aire que me encierra!
Y anclar otra vez en la nada.
La noche es mi madre y mi hermana,
la nada es mi patria lejana,
la nada llena de silencio,
la nada llena de vacío,
la nada sin tiempo ni frío,
la nada en que no pasa nada.

TO GO BACK...

To go back to the distant country,
to go back to the forgotten country,
secretly deformed
by exile in this land.
To leave the air that encases me!
To anchor once again in nothing.
Night is my mother and my sister,
nothing is my distant country,
the nothing full of silence,
the nothing full of emptiness,
the nothing with no time, no cold,
the nothing where nothing happens.

DÉCIMA MUERTE

a Ricardo de Alcázar

I

¡Qué prueba de la existencia
habrá mayor que la suerte
de estar viviendo sin verte
y muriendo en tu presencia!
Esta lúcida conciencia
de amar a lo nunca visto
y de esperar lo imprevisto;
este caer sin llegar
es la anguistia de pensar
que puesto que muero existo.

II

Si en todas partes estás,
en el agua y en la tierra,
en el aire que me encierra
y en el incendio voraz;
y si a todas partes vas
conmigo en el pensamiento,
en el soplo de mi aliento
y en mi sangre confundida,
¿no serás, Muerte, en mi vida,
agua, fuego, polvo y viento?

III

Si tienes manos, que sean
de un tacto sutil y blando,
apenas sensible cuando
anestesiado me crean;
y que tus ojos me vean
sin mirarme, de tal suerte
que nada me desconcierte
ni tu vista ni tu roce,

DEATH IN DÉCIMAS

for Ricardo de Alcázar

I

There's no proof of existence
that is greater than this fate:
living without seeing you
and dying in your presence!
This limpid recognition:
loving what's never been seen
and waiting for the unseen;
this falling with no landing
is the anguish of thinking
given I die I exist.

II

If you are there everywhere,
on land and in the water,
in the air encasing me
and in voracious fire;
if you go there everywhere,
traveling with me in my thoughts,
in the heaving of my breath
and in my blood's disarray,
are you not, Death, in my life,
water, fire, dust and wind?

III

If you have hands, let them be
of a soft and subtle touch,
scarcely sensitive as they
anesthetized create me;
let your eyes as they watch me
without seeing, be such that
nothing will bewilder me,
neither your glances nor your touch,

para no sentir un goce
ni un dolor contigo, Muerte.

IV

Por caminos ignorados,
por hendiduras secretas,
por las misteriosas vetas
de troncos recién cortados,
te ven mis ojos cerrados
entrar en mi alcoba oscura
a conventir mi envoltura
opaca, febril, cambiante,
en materia de diamante
luminosa, eterna y pura.

V

No duermo para que al verte
llegar lenta y apagada,
para que al oír pausada
tu voz que silencios vierte,
para que al tocar la nada
que envuelve tu cuerpo yerto,
para que a tu olor desierto
pueda, sin sombra de sueño,
saber que de ti me adueño,
sentir que muero despierto.

VI

La aguja del instantero
recorrerá su cuadrante,
todo cabrá en un instante
del espacio verdadero
que, ancho, profundo y señero,
será elástico a tu paso
de modo que el tiempo cierto
prolongará nuestro abrazo

so that I will feel no pain,
feel no pleasure with you, Death.

IV

Down the unknown pathways,
through the hidden fissures,
through the mysterious veins
of trunks newly sawn apart,
my closed eyes are watching you
come into my dark bedroom
to change this earthly trapping,
opaque, restless and unfixed,
into a stuff of diamonds,
shining, eternal and pure.

V

Not sleeping so I'll see you
coming in, slow and subdued,
so I'll hear your hesitant
voice that spills with silence,
so that touching the nothing
that surrounds your stiff body,
so that your deserted smell,
without the shadow of sleep,
will know I am your master,
will feel that I die awake.

VI

The sweep-hand of the instant
will race across its quadrant,
everything will be contained
in a moment of true space
so wide and deep and alone,
elastic to your footstep,
in a manner that fixed time
will so prolong our embrace

y será posible, acaso,
vivir después de haber muerto.

VII

En el roce, en el contacto,
en la inefable delicia
de la suprema caricia
que desemboca en el acto,
hay un misterioso pacto
del espasmo delirante
en que un cielo alucinante
y un infierno de agonía
se funden cuando eres mía
y soy tuyo en un instante.

VIII

¡Hasta en la ausencia estás viva!
Porque te encuentro en el hueco
de una forma y en el eco
de una nota fugitiva;
porque en mi propia saliva
fundes tu sabor sombrío,
y a cambio de lo que es mío
me dejas sólo el temor
de hallar hasta en el sabor
la presencia del vacío.

IX

Si te llevo en mí prendida
y te acaricio y escondo;
si te alimento en el fondo
de mi más secreta herida;
si mi muerte te da vida
y goce mi frenesí,
¿qué será, Muerte, de ti

it may just be possible
to live after having died.

VII

In the touch, in the friction,
in the nameless delight
of the ultimate caress
that empties out in the act,
there's a mysterious pact
in the delirious spasm;
hallucinated heaven
and a hell of slow dying
become one when you are mine
and in the instant I'm yours.

VIII

Even absent you're alive!
I find you in the hollow
of a form and the echo
of some momentary sound;
even my own saliva
tastes of your shadowy taste,
and in exchange for what's mine
you've left me only the fear
of finding even in taste
the presence of this void.

IX

If I keep you imprisoned,
and caress you and hide you;
if I feed you in the depths
of my most intimate wound,
if my death gives you your life
and my frenzy such delights,
what will become of you, Death,

cuando al salir yo del mundo,
deshecho el nudo profundo,
tengas que salir de mí?

X

En vano amenazas, Muerte,
cerrar la boca a mi herida
y poner fin a mi vida
con una palabra inerte.
¡Qué puedo pensar al verte,
si en mi angustia verdadera
tuve que violar la espera;
si en vista de tu tardanza
para llenar mi esperanza
no hay hora en que yo no muera!

when, when I must leave this world,
untying this tangled knot,
you too will have to leave me?

X

In vain you threaten me, Death,
closing your mouth on my wound,
putting an end to my life
with a lugubrious word.
What can I think, seeing you,
if, with my actual dying
I had to end this waiting,
if in sight of your slowness
in fulfilling all my hopes
there's no time when I'm not dying!

Décimas: stanzas of ten octosyllables with the rhyme scheme abba:
ac: cddc. The translation has seven-syllable lines and is unrhymed.

HIEROGLYPHS OF

DESIRE

Octavio Paz

TRANSLATED BY ESTHER ALLEN

Why is it that all those who have become
eminent in philosophy or politics or poetry
or the arts are clearly of an atrabilious
temperament and some of them to such an
extent as to be affected by diseases
caused by black bile?

– ARISTOTLE
Problems, XXX
(Translated by E.S. Forster)

XAVIER WITH AN X

IN 1931, WHILE I was still a student at the National Preparatory School, some friends and I edited a small literary magazine called *Barandal* [Balustrade]. We came up with the idea of publishing, as a separate supplement to each issue, poems and texts by writers we admired, such as Alfonso Reyes, Carlos Pellicer, Xavier Villaurrutia, and Salvador Novo. We wrote them, proposing the idea, and, remarkably enough, they all accepted. This led to our first meeting with Novo who, in those days, was director of the Ministry of Public Education's Editorial Department, issuing his orders from an office on the Ministry's ground floor. Working under him, in a miniscule space which also served as the waiting room, were Xavier Villaurrutia and Efrén Hernández. Tall, his shoulders a bit stooped, already slightly obese, Novo reigned over his two friends and subordinates with an indefinable mixture of courtesy and insolence. He wore the light-colored, loose-fitting suits that were fashionable at the time, and looked more like the powerful executive of an American company than a Mexican dandy. In that Mexico, still full of remnants of the nineteenth century, Novo's assertion of the will to be modern was almost defiant. We were stunned by his ties, his irreverent opinions, his beige shoes that were rounded at the toe, his slicked-back hair, his plucked eyebrows, his Anglicisms. His mission was to astonish or to irritate, and he succeeded.

Villaurrutia and Hernández were both slender, fragile, and short of stature. All resemblance between them ended there. Efrén Hernández would pop out from among the papers and books on his enormous desk, a smiling face with the features of a frightened rodent. Behind his glasses, a pair of lively, ironic eyes were watching. He dressed like a notary's clerk, and had a little, cracked voice that would suddenly become sharp and metallic like the screech of a toy train going around a curve. He was the persona of his stories: intelligent, shy, reticent, lost in circumlocutions that led to paradoxes, falsely modest, extravagant, and, more than distracted – abstracted, revolving around a certainty that was hidden but whose appearance was imminent. Novo was deliberately brilliant; Hernández deliberately opaque. Villaurrutia did not pretend to be humble or lower his head: he raised it and moved it from left to right and from right to left, between curiosity and disdain. A bird surveying its territory and defining its boundaries. Like Novo he was elegant; unlike him he strove for discretion. His suits were dark grey or dark blue. When he walked, he held his gaze high, and his footsteps rang out forcefully. His shirts were immaculately white and too large for him, which accentuated the slenderness of his neck. Matte skin, thin lips, a nose with wide nostrils – a physiognomy which would have been rather ordinary if not for the liquid eyes, large and dark beneath strict brows, and the noble amplitude of the forehead. His hair was black with a slight wave.

The first time I spoke with him, I realized that he knew how to listen. Even more: he knew how to answer. Two virtues that are rare, especially among writers. He spoke unhurriedly. At times this quality became a defect: you could see him listening to himself. From the beginning I was surprised by his beautiful voice, grave and flowing like a dark river. His manners were sober and exact. There were two constant notes, one a spur, the other a brake: courtesy, and an irony that was sometimes cruel. Years later I discovered that his good manners concealed an irritable temperament; the epigrams he shot off defended an insecure and anguished being, prone to depressions and losses of will. Though he was not what is called a natural person, it seemed to me that, unlike Novo and Hernández, he was not playing at being his persona. Or rather, he, too, like anyone who is out of the ordinary, was a persona, but his features coincided with his mask. When he gave us the poems for *Barandal,* he insisted that the *plaquette* be bound in wallpaper. He himself chose the brand, the paper and the colors. More than a confession, it was a definition. Green and gold on black: colors as nocturnal as his poetry. *Tapisserie:* the poem conceived as a closed form, a verbal chamber whose walls are pages – and whose pages are doors suddenly opening onto a corridor that ends in a gulf of shadow.

Those first encounters with Villaurrutia were superficial and I wouldn't remember them at all if they hadn't been the beginning of a closer association. Some years later, in January 1937, a small book of mine, *Raíz del hombre* [The Root of Men], came out, and my friend Jorge Cuesta wrote an article on it for the first issue of *Letras de México* [Mexican Letters]. Cuesta's review was not much to the liking of certain of his friends, who took a dim view both of my poems and of my political opinions. In the same issue of *Letras de México,* and on the same page, was an unsigned review in which a poem of mine was harshly judged. I learned later that it had been written by Bernardo Ortiz de Montellano. Shortly thereafter, Jorge invited me to lunch and mentioned, with no explanation, that several other friends of his would be joining us. I accepted and we arranged that I would drop by the office where he worked as a chemist for a sugar company. When I arrived, I ran into Xavier Villaurrutia in the lobby. He told me that he and Cuesta were taking me to the lunch, and gave me the names of the others who would be there: the group known as the *Contemporáneos* [Contemporaries] in its entirety. I suddenly realized that I had been invited to a sort of initiation ceremony, or, rather, to an examination: I was to be examined and Xavier and Jorge would act as my mentors.

We took a taxi to a restaurant called The Swan that faced one of the entrances to Chapultepec Park, near the flower market. I well remember who was there: Ortiz de Montellano, José and Celestino Gorostiza, Samuel Ramos, Octavio G. Barreda, Jaime Torres Bodet, Enrique González Rojo, Elías Nandino and Father Mendoza. Only three were missing: Carlos Pellicer, Novo and Gilberto Owen (who was then living in Colombia). We spoke of the opposing ideas of Goethe and Valéry on poetic translation, but, above all, we spoke of Gide, Communism and the writer. Those were the days of the Spanish Civil War. All of them sided with the Republicans, but all of them were opposed to the idea of the writer's *engagement* and loathed the "socialist realism" that had been proclaimed the aesthetic doctrine of Communism. They questioned me at length on the contradiction they thought they had discerned between my political opinions and my poetic tastes. I answered as best I could. If my dialectic didn't convince them, my sincerity must have impressed them, for they invited me to their monthly lunches. But I was unable to attend their meetings; soon after that lunch I left Mexico City for a long time – first to the Yucatán and later to Spain. My connection with Villaurrutia was interrupted once more.

When I returned, in 1938, Xavier and Octavio G. Barreda invited me to their *tertulia,* or literary gathering, at the Café Paris. The Café Paris had two eras. During the first, which I did not know, the café was located on calle de Gante, and was frequented by Cuesta, Luis Cardoza y Aragón, Xavier, José Gorostiza and, when he was in Mexico, Antonin Artaud. In my time, the Café Paris was on calle 5 de Mayo. The group met between three and four in the afternoon every day except Saturday and Sunday. Those who attended most assiduously were Barreda, Xavier, Samuel Ramos, the painter Orozco Romero, Carlos Luquín, and Celestino Gorostiza. Two Spaniards arrived a year later: José Moreno Villa and León Felipe. Also in attendance, though less frequently, were José Gorostiza, Cuesta, Elías Nandino, Ortiz de Montellano, and Alí Chumacero, among others. At the same time, but at a different table, a group of writers of a more or less Marxist bent would meet. Then, as the afternoon ended, another group, more colorful and tumultuous than the preceding two, arrived, which included various notable women – María Izquierdo, Lola Alvarez Bravo, Lupe Marín, Lya Kostakowsky – and young artists and poets like Juan Soriano and Neftalí Beltrán.

At our table, literary and political gossip was exchanged and discussed: the significance of the words *happiness* and *democracy* in Whitman, realism in its fantastic and socialist varieties, *cante jondo* and Biblical versicles . . . During a certain period we amused ourselves by giving the titles of books, slightly deformed, to people and situations. A writer of short stature who was going out with a blonde of eminent proportions was instantly dubbed *Tartarín in the Alps.* The cane belonging to The Gentleman (as Xavier referred to him in one of his epigrams) was transformed little by little into a prehensile organ like Fourier's *archibras.* The saga of The Gentleman and his Cane contained memorable episodes: with his Cane, The Gentleman held up the roof of his house the night of the earthquake, and with his Cane he tested the temperature of his bath every morning.

We would leave the Café Paris and go out into the already inhospitable city of Mexico with our hearts pounding rapidly – whether from the excess of caffeine or from the anguish all of us felt to a greater or lesser degree, I don't know. Sometimes we'd go for a walk through the city. While Barreda announced the imminent death of literature, Xavier continued, undisturbed, to speak of Rilke's French poems or of

Whitman as a poet for Boy Scouts, which always provoked León Felipe's wrath. Night was falling, the friends would disperse, and all the intelligent, impassioned, or ironic words would be no more than a little air, blown away at the turn of a corner. I felt that I was walking among ruins, that the passers-by were phantoms. From those years came the sonnets I called *Crepúsculos de la ciudad* [Twilights in the City] in homage and in response to Lugones, but also to Xavier Villaurrutia:

> Stretched out at my feet, I see myself in the steel
> of the worn stone and the asphalt:
> opaque mechanical corpses step
> not on my shadow, but on my body itself.[1]

In 1938, thanks to Alfonso Reyes, the Buenos Aires publishing house Sur brought out Villaurrutia's central work: *Nostalgia for Death*. José Bianco, the secretary of *Sur* magazine, told Xavier to entrust the review they would publish to the Mexican writer of his choice, and Xavier asked me to write it. Thus began my work with *Sur* and my friendship with Bianco. The afternoons in the Café Paris brought me into collaboration with Xavier and together we undertook several literary enterprises, the most notable of which were the founding of the literary magazine *El Hijo Pródigo* [The Prodigal Son] and the compilation of *Laurel*, an anthology of modern Spanish poetry. The editorial board of *El Hijo Pródigo*, led by Octavio G. Barreda, united two generations, that of the Contemporáneos and my own, the generation of the magazines *Taller* [Workshop] and *Tierra Nueva* [New Earth]. Both groups shared certain moral and aesthetic attitudes that, above and beyond certain political and literary changes, were essentially the same as those later sustained by the *Revista Méxicana de Literatura* [Mexican Review of Literature] (in both of its eras), the authentic *Plural*, and *Vuelta* [Return]. The situation at that time was not very different from the situation now: *El Hijo Pródigo*, especially in its first issues, was a polemical magazine that defended the liberty of the imagination against the

---

[1] *Yazgo a mis pies, me miro en el acero*
de la piedra gastada y del asfalto:
pisan opacos muertos maquinales
no mi sombra, mi cuerpo verdadero.

confusion between art and propaganda.

The outcry that *Laurel* provoked was even more violent than the one that had greeted *El Hijo Pródigo,* but this is not the occasion for retelling the story of that scandal. It was my idea to put together the anthology. With it, I wanted to demonstrate the continuity and unity of the poetry of our language. It was an act of faith. I believed (and still believe) that a poetic tradition is not defined by the political concept of nationality but by a language and by the relationships that are woven between styles and creators. It is strange, and as true of Xavier's generation as of my own, that despite having professed the doctrine of change and rupture – or perhaps because of it – we have always been preoccupied with the idea of continuity. I spoke with José Bergamín, who was head of the publishing house Séneca, proposed the book to him and told him I couldn't do it alone. He accepted my idea immediately and asked if I had a collaborator in mind. No, I hadn't thought of anyone in particular, but at that moment Villaurrutia's name came into my head. Bergamín accepted that idea, too, and also suggested two Spanish poets: Emilio Prados and Juan Gil Albert. Two generations of Spaniards and Mexicans: Villaurrutia/Prados and Gil Albert/Paz.

From the beginning Xavier directed our work. Every evening he and I saw each other, at times in the Iberoamerican Library on calle de Luis González Obregón and at other times in the Séneca offices. The work consisted first in choosing the poets who would figure in the anthology, and then in choosing the poems and writing the biographical and bibliographical notes. Emilio Prados was not present at these meetings; his contribution was limited to the selection of his own poems. Gil Albert was full of good will, but since he was barely acquainted with Latin American poetry he couldn't be of much use to us in our selection of poets born in the Americas. He did participate in the selection of the Spanish poets, however, and in the selection of poems.

The title of the anthology and the epigraph by Lope de Vega ("captured in laurel the fugitive plant") were both Bergamín's idea. In the end, shortly before sending the manuscript to the printer, Bergamín suggested we leave certain poets out (Larrea, Dámaso Alonso), a suggestion we had the weakness to accept. Also at the last minute, Villaurrutia and Bergamín decided, with Prados's approval – this was his only participation – to eliminate the group of young poets that made up the fourth section of the anthology (Miguel Hernández, Juan Gil Albert, Luis Rosales, José Lezama Lima, myself, and others I can't recall). I was opposed to this and Gil Albert was with me. They paid no attention to us. Xavier's prologue alludes, not without a certain irony, to this incident: "The first group of poets in this anthology has been succeeded by at least – for a new group is forming, agitated and impatient – two others . . . " The agitated and impatient element was us. Pablo Neruda, however, was not indignant over the exclusion of Miguel Hernández, as he would later write in his *Canto general,* but over the inclusion of Vicente Huidobro. Now, after so many years, I think that Bergamín and Villaurrutia were right: except in the case of Miguel Hernández, the inclusion of poets who in those years were "the youngest generation" was premature.

At the end of 1943 I left Mexico for many years. At first, Barreda and several other friends wrote to me. Then, nothing. The great Mexican silence. Once in a while I had word of Xavier, though never directly. But in 1949 I published *Libertad bajo palabra* [Freedom on Parole] and sent him a copy of it. A few months later I received his *Canto a la primavera y otros poemas* [Song to the Spring and Other Poems] with an inscription so generous and effusive that it still moves me. Among the good things that have happened to me are those lines by Xavier. But after the good always comes the bad. One morning in 1950, I ran into Rufino Tamayo in the Mexican Embassy in Paris. He greeted me gravely and said: "Have you heard the news? Xavier Villaurrutia died." As is often the case at such moments, I heard Rufino's words without hearing them. I felt nothing. A few hours later, when I was alone, I realized what they really signified. But I am wrong to speak of *significance:* death has none and that is what leaves us defenseless before it. Confronted with what says nothing, we can say nothing. Death is the universal non-significance, the great refutation of our languages and our reasonings.

During those years in Paris I sometimes thought of my eventual return to Mexico and in my head I would repeat the verses by Tablada dedicated to López Velarde: "How sad the evening will be, / when you are back in Mexico / without seeing . . . X.V." I finally returned, nine years later. A different Mexico. New friends: Carlos Fuentes, Jorge Portilla, Ramón and Ana Xirau, Elena Poniatowska, Jaime García

Terrés. At some event or gathering I saw Elías Nandino. We spoke and remembered Xavier. Ever generous, he sent me a package a week later. It was a small book with red covers. I opened it to find that it was the copy of *Libertad bajo palabra* I had sent Xavier years before. Xavier had had it bound and had carefully annotated it. On the last page, he had written, in his small, light handwriting, a poem of four lines, probably one of the last he ever wrote: "Palabra" [Word]. I read it as an oblique commentary on my book—and on poetry:

> Word, you don't know what you name.
> Word, proud queen!
> You give the name of cloud to the fugitive shadow
> of a world where the clouds are shadows.[2]

FOR SEVERAL YEARS I saw Xavier two or three times a week. Was I his friend? We never used the familiar *tu* in speaking to each other, he never invited me to his house, and he didn't come to my house more than two or three times. Though he was a Francophile, his reserve was Spanish or, more precisely, Hispano-Arabic. Rarely will a Muslim invite you to his house. The same thing happens (or happened) in Spain: friends see each other in a café. Guillermo de Torre tells of the astonishment he and the young Spanish poets of his day felt when Vicente Huidobro, during his stay in Madrid in 1918, invited them to his house and introduced them to his wife. Xavier's reserve was quite a contrast to Novo's swagger. While Novo was rather ostentatious about his sexual inclinations, Xavier was protective of his private life. I don't believe this was hypocrisy. He wasn't in hiding and was capable of confronting public condemnation. He was as discreet in real life as in literature; his love of form was reflected as much in his way of dressing as in his hendecasyllables. For him, excessive brilliance was the mortal sin.

Xavier was one of the last representatives of a certain bourgeois Mexican morality whose extinction was brought about by the double

---

[2] *Palabra que no sabes lo que nombras.*
Palabra, ¡reina altiva!
Llamas nube a la sombra fugitiva
de un mundo en que las nubes son las sombras.

erosion of "Americanism" and the peasant mores of the new plutoc-racy. This morality, based more on manners than on precepts, closer to aesthetics than to ethics, can be summed up in a single word: de-cency. The origin of the attitude *decency* designates is triple: Arab, Spanish, and Indian. Three hierarchical traditions, three societies ob-sessed with rank. Decency is the morality of the upper middle class: prudence, circumspection, protection of intimacy and, fundamen-tally, great pride and great fear of what people will say. Not honor in the Spaniard's sense of the word, but rather, decorum.

My relationship with Xavier was, like the relationship I had with Cuesta, of an intellectual nature. Or rather: of a literary nature. Xavier was not as interested in ideas as Cuesta and I were. All theories, sys-tems, and schools of thought inspired him with an invincible distrust. The horror he felt when confronted with Marxism, Thomism, and other systems diminished into impatience and irony where poetic schools and movements such as Surrealism were concerned. He was not a man of ideas: he was an extraordinarily intelligent man who had decided, out of scepticism, to employ his intelligence in the service of his sensibility. He did not want to think or judge, he wanted to plumb the depths of his sensations and sentiments, with lucidity. Though it did not bring him true spiritual wealth, this voluntary limitation did give him something essential which cannot easily be condensed into a phrase. When he contemplated the complexity of sensations and pas-sions, he discovered that there are secret corridors running between dreaming and wakefulness, love and hate, absence and presence. The best of his work is an exploration of these corridors.

His scepticism was born not only from reflection but also from his temperament. He fled from extremes and was fascinated by them. There was a continuous oscillation between intense, electrical states of mind bordering on exasperation, and prostration, inertia, indifference; irritability and melancholy; brief outbursts and prolonged lethargies. His description of López Velarde's poetry suits him admirably – not his work, but his temperament: restless, never solidly grounded any-where, making a leap and landing in a paradox, inhabiting an affirma-tion suspended over the void. Not intellectual doubt, but vital anxiety.

Xavier's scepticism, like that of the other members of his genera-tion, had a social origin as well. It was a reaction to certain experiences of life in Mexico. As children, they had witnessed the violence and the killings of the Revolution; as young men, they had watched the rapid corruption of the revolutionaries and their transformation into an uncouth and avid plutocracy. The previous generation could still delude themselves. But the Contemporáneos could no longer believe in the revolutionaries or in their programs, so they isolated themselves in a private world, populated by the phantoms of eroticism, dreaming, and death. A world that was ruled by the word *absence*. At some point I dropped by the "studio" Xavier kept in the center of the city to pick up a book. I was surprised by the room's atmosphere: it looked like a set for one of Cocteau's films (*The Blood of the Poet*). He saw that I was surprised and told me, "I've had to construct this artificial refuge for myself in order to endure Mexico."

The stance of Xavier and his friends was what we now call *interior exile*. How many writers has Mexico condemned to live as exiles in their own land? After many years of absence, Alfonso Reyes returns to his old school, San Ildefonso – which Xavier and I also attended – and says of his memories:

> I was another, being the same:
> I was he who wanted to leave.
> To go back is to weep. I do not regret
> the wide world. I am not he who came back
> but my enslaved feet.[3]

"Others" – the men and women of "all classes" with whom we speak, whose paths we cross, day after day, in streets, offices, churches, buses – do not appear in any of the work produced by the Contemporáneos. In Pellicer's work there are mountains, rivers, trees, and ruins, there are stereotypical heroes and villains, but there are no people. There were two opposing, but fundamentally similar, ways of doing away with "others": in Novo's work people became the object

---

[3] *Yo era otro, siendo el mismo:*
yo era el que quiere irse.
Volver es sollozar. No estoy arrepentido
del ancho mundo. No soy yo quien vuelve
sino mis pies esclavos.

of derision and mockery, while in Torres Bodet they were the subject of edifying and commonplace allegories. In the poems of Gorostiza, Villaurrutia, and Ortiz de Montellano no one is there: everyone and everything has become a reflection, a ghost. Let me explain this by citing two very different poets, Eliot and Apollinaire. People are the city, and the city is the double face of the people who inhabit it, the nocturnal face and the diurnal. People: at once real and unreal. In "Un fantôme de nuées" [Phantom of the Clouds], Apollinaire describes a street scene with acrobats and the astonishment of the onlookers when a circus boy disappears among his pirouettes, swallowed by his leap. Afterwards

> The saltimbanques lifted the great dumb-bells in their arms
> And juggled with the weights
>
> But each spectator looked in himself for the miraculous child
> Century O century of clouds[4]

Eliot's vision of the city was not only different, it was the opposite. But people appear in Eliot's vision, too, and, again, the real is unreal, the unreal real:

> Unreal City
> Under the brown fog of a winter noon
> Mr. Eugenides, the Smyrna merchant...

The city is people and people are our horizon. The poetry of the Contemporáneos, though admirable for many reasons, lacks this horizon. A poetry with wings but without the weight – the nightmare – of history. The essayists of the group did confront the fact of living in Mexico in this century; with them began the moral critique we desperately need. But Cuesta, the most profoundly talented of them, died too young, and Ramos did not go far enough.

Despite their solitude, all of them worked for the Mexican Government. Economic necessity does not entirely explain their attitude.

---

[4] Trans. Roger Shattuck in *Selected Writings of Guillaume Apollinaire*.

They had to leave their official positions in 1932 after the *Examen* [Inquiry] scandal. *Examen* was a magazine founded and edited by Jorge Cuesta. It lasted a scant three issues: the publication of two chapters of a novel by Rubén Salazar Mallén which contained "obscene expressions" caused an outcry among various ultramontane journalists barricaded behind the newspaper *Excelsior*. Many of the Contemporáneos were functionaries of the Ministry of Public Education. The attack on them in the name of morality and good manners was really directed against the Minister of Education, Bassols, who was hated by the reactionaries. To evade the attack, Bassols decided not to defend his associates. *Examen* was taken before the courts and the defendants, Cuesta and Salazar Mallén, found themselves facing a long trial. "For the first time in Mexico," as Luis Mario Schneider has observed, "a group of writers and a literary magazine were on trial." In the end, Cuesta and Salazar Mallén were acquitted. But all the while – as Villaurrutia wrote in a letter to Eduardo Luquín – "Bassols did not show his face." José Gorostiza, Ramos, Pellicer, and Villaurrutia himself were left without their posts in the Ministry of Public Education. No less serious than the bureaucratic retaliation was the hostility of the press. "*Examen* will not survive this," Villaurrutia said in the same letter, "and we are condemned to expressing ourselves orally for a while. In the newspapers, we are boycotted by the ill-bred breed of journalists." The persecution didn't last long; a few months later they were all working for the government again, not in Public Education, but in Foreign Affairs and other ministries. Cuesta began his association with the newspaper *El Universal*, and the rest became involved with various other magazines. *Examen* was their last undertaking as a group. It was also the most lucid and rigorous thing they ever did. The magazines that succeeded *Examen* were either the official organs of younger groups (*Taller, Tierra Nueva*) or eclectic publications (*Letras de México*).

The second and most violent campaign against the Contemporáneos happened during the regime of President Cárdenas. On that occasion the attack came not from the conservatives but from the revolutionaries; it was not, as in the case of *Excelsior,* an attack on the Government: it was an attack by the Government. It was an assault on free literature as well as an expression of resentment by mediocre, opportunistic writers and artists. Once again, vengeance wore the mask of ideology.

Various members of the Chamber of Deputies, along with a chorus of Fine Arts Academy functionaries and "progressive" writers, denounced them as reactionaries and called them precious, decadent, and cosmopolitan. Almost all the Contemporáneos – except, as I recall, Torres Bodet and Ortiz de Montellano – had to leave their government posts once more. Since the country had grown, it wasn't hard for them to find employment in the private sphere – advertising, cinema – and earn a comfortable living. Even Novo prospered and became a kind of minor Aretino, albeit richer than his Renaissance predecessor. Xavier made his living teaching and writing book and theatre reviews and the prologues to the books published by Cultura. But as soon as they could go back to work for the government, all of them did. Was this because of some Hispanic mania for public office? In part. It can also be blamed on the idea, Hispanic as well, that power is the sun of public life. Among us, the State has immense prestige: we are the heirs of Spanish patrimonialism and French centralism. In our system of values, wealth and knowledge come after power. Mexican children dream of being presidents, not bankers. Every Mexican city, every town, every municipality, and every home reproduces a structure of domination that comes to us from pre-Hispanic society and that was preserved by the Spaniards.

Jorge Cuesta pointed out that criticism was the distinctive characteristic of his group: "Even if they cannot be called critics, almost all of them have adopted a critical attitude." Nonetheless, with the exceptions already mentioned – Cuesta, and, to a limited extent, Ramos – it was a generation that did not exercise its critical faculties in the areas where we need them most: morality and politics. Novo was a brilliant and venal satirist; the rest preferred action and bureaucracy, in silence. But there is a positive aspect to their attitude. In Mexico, the State represents the nation more manifestly than in other countries; it would not be an exaggeration to say that modern Mexico, in large measure, is the creation of the Mexican State. The agent of historical and social evolution in Mexico has, until very recently, been the State, not the bourgeoisie. It is natural for the best members of a society such as ours to aspire to be public servants. Torres Bodet and José Gorostiza held very high positions and both of them contributed to the construction of the modern Mexican State. Torres Bodet's vocation was that of a *gran com-*

mis de l'Etat, a sort of Colbert without a Louis XIV, or rather, with the synthetic Louis XIV that is El Señor Presidente. When the history of Mexico's international politics in that period is written, the enormous influence exerted by José Gorostiza will be discovered, an influence that was not transformed into political power because it was limited to ideas and strategy. He was a true counsellor of Princes, more in the tradition of Confucius than of Machiavelli.

The Contemporáneos' attitude may appear contradictory. It is not. As cosmopolitan as they could be where art was concerned, they were nonetheless ardent patriots. Patriotic declarations are constant, though somewhat diffused, throughout their works, along with a more or less veiled satire of foreigners. If, for example, you reread some of Villaurrutia's plays, where the foreigners are mainly Spaniards and North Americans, you will find that *foreigner* is a synonym for *intruder*. His Francophilia, as Cuesta said many times, was the free choice not of a (French) particularity, but of a universalism. Whether the French tradition indeed represents the universal vision of man that the Contemporáneos saw in it could be debated; it is, however, indisputable that for them Francophilia was a profession of universalist faith. For that reason it could coexist with their patriotism. Their Mexicanism, in sharp contrast to Diego Rivera's, was neither colorful nor folkloric, it was another form of the *decorum* I mentioned previously.

It was a grotesque error: they were obstinate, fervent patriots and were persecuted as cosmopolitans and lovers of everything foreign. The strangest thing about it was that the attacks in the name of nationalism came from writers who called themselves Marxists. The confusion between Marxism and nationalism has been and is one of the expressions of the obscurantism of our time, especially in Latin America. Xavier's Mexicanism was not an idea, which is why I don't call it nationalism; it was a feeling, a tradition. His attitude towards Spaniards was inherited from the hostility that the criollos of New Spain felt towards them, a hostility which increased during the Wars of Independence and the nineteenth century. If I'm not mistaken, he composed, in collaboration with Usigli, several epigrams against the Spanish intellectuals who had taken refuge in Mexico, especially José Bergamín who was reproached, among other things, for certain rather disparaging comments he had written years before regarding Juan Ruiz de

Alarcón. Alarcón's hunchback, into which Lope, Quevedo, and Mira de Amescua had stuck their banderillas like so many picadors, kindled another literary war three centuries later in the cafés of Mexico. The epigrams, printed on pink paper, were circulated everywhere. Bergamín responded with some ferocious sonnets. It was the perfect remedy: a truce was called, followed by a general amnesty.

After that, Xavier's hostility towards Spaniards was attenuated, but not his impatience with our government's attitude. One day, during a short trip we took to Jalapa, he confided to me: "I'm not – how could I be? – opposed to granting exile to political refugees. Nor am I opposed to giving them aid. And how could I deny that many of the exiled Spanish intellectuals are worthy people? What irritates me is the preferential treatment that the semiliterates who govern this country give to mediocre foreigners, while disdaining so many distinguished Mexicans. I don't subscribe to any political ideology, but I would like our Government to practice an intelligent nationalism, in other words, to help and stimulate intelligent Mexicans." I answered that he was postulating a logical impossibility: an intelligent nationalism. He didn't like my answer.

Like all artists and writers – which is to say: like all people of sensitivity, intelligence, and imagination – the Contemporáneos found it difficult to conform to conventions and social expectations, especially those imposed by bourgeois society, far more rigid and hypocritical than the aristocratic society it replaced. But it is one thing to be original or even eccentric in one's conduct or opinions; it is another thing altogether to criticize society. Singularly timid in matters of philosophy and politics, the Contemporáneos could not be called either revolutionaries or conservatives. It would be useless to search their lives and works for declarations, ideas, or attitudes resembling those of the French Surrealists or of Pound and Eliot. The homosexuality of certain of the Contemporáneos (Novo, Pellicer, Villaurrutia) is no secret. They were honest with themselves about it, and confronted intolerance with integrity and humor. Nonetheless, the moral independence and intellectual coherence of a Gide or the rebellion of a Luis Cernuda cannot be found in their work.

I have touched on the subject of morality and politics because it is intimately linked to that of poetry and art. Obviously, I do not intend to subject literature to the precepts of morality or to the necessities of political strategy. On the contrary: if I feel indebted to the Contemporáneos, if I am in any way their heir, it is precisely because of their brave and intransigent defense of the freedom of art and culture. But if these pages are to be a critical description of Mexican culture at a given moment, how can I keep from mentioning their insensitivity to certain subjects which, from their time to the present, have preoccupied and disturbed most of the writers in the world? In 1938, in a brief text (titled "Reason for Being") that appeared in the second issue of *Taller*, I acknowledged everything that joined us to the Contemporáneos, but I also pointed out everything that separated us from them. The Contemporáneos's project was to incorporate the modern tradition; they carried on the work initiated by the *modernistas* and continued by the writers of the *Ateneo*. Their interpretation of the European tradition was no more rigorous or extensive than Reyes's interpretation, but it was more daring. They wanted to be the contemporaries of the writers of their time and, in large measure, they succeeded. However, their interpretation of the modern tradition disdained the visionary and passional element that from Romanticism to Surrealism has been one of its essential components. The poetry of sleep and dreaming, of oneiric images, leads to the idea of subversion. The poets of the twentieth century, like the Romantics before them, moved from vision to subversion, and from there to politics. In the English language, as I have tried to show in *Children of the Mire,* there was an inverse but symmetrical evolution: North American poets were, like the Surrealists and the Latin Americans, prey to the double fascination of politics and religion (or of the "other religion": the hermetic tradition). The words *religion* and *reaction* are intimately joined to the poetry of Eliot and Pound, just as *magic* and *revolution* are inseparable from that of Breton, Eluard, and Aragon. The Contemporáneos were indifferent to all of these words, and it was precisely this indifference that separated us from them. To give an example: Surrealism was, for them, an exclusively aesthetic experience; for us, automatic writing and the world of dreams were at once a poetic and an ethic, a vision and a subversion. Two words shook us to the core, but left them entirely unmoved: *rebellion* and *revelation*.

The "contemporariness" of the Contemporáneos was incomplete; their interpretation of the modern poetic tradition failed to take in the bundle of oppositions which constitutes its modernity. But in those years the Guatemalan poet Luis Cardoza y Aragón arrived in Mexico. He was almost the same age as the Contemporáneos, he had been living in Europe, his first book had been praised by Ramón Gómez de la Serna and he had a first-hand acquaintance with the European avant-garde, especially with Surrealism. In his poems and his beliefs the two halves that had seemed fatally irreconcilable to me and to Efraín Huerta were united and inseparable: vision and subversion, rebellion and revelation. Cardoza y Aragón's activity was isolated and marginal, and, for those very reasons, decisive. On the one hand, he was very close to the Contemporáneos; not only was he friendly with Cuesta, Gorostiza, and Villaurrutia, but his poetic and pictorial tastes were similar to theirs. On the other hand, his political and moral sympathies inclined him towards the ideas defended by the writers and artists who would, a little later, found the LEAR (League of Revolutionary Writers and Artists). I still remember the night when Huerta, José Revueltas, and I, in a room at the LEAR building, faced with a hostile public and the anathema of several bishops and their coadjutors, heard Cardoza y Aragón defend poetry, not as an activity in the service of the Revolution, but as the expression of perpetual human subversion. Cardoza y Aragón was the bridge between the avant-garde and the poets of my generation. He was more than a bridge – he joined two oppositions. But it was not long before the unity of poetic and revolutionary activity had ended in discord. The twentieth century's political religion has been no more tolerant than the sixteenth century's religious politics. This conflict, which is central not only to the history of my generation but to the entirety of modern poetry, did not affect any of the Contemporáneos. With extraordinary clarity, Cuesta saw the opposition: "There is an abyss between the spirit that recognizes the subversive power of the word and the spirit that sees its revolutionary utility only in the renunciation of that power." He saw it, but he did not live it.

IT IS IMPOSSIBLE to reduce Xavier Villaurrutia's vital and spiritual attitudes to a doctrine. He once told me that he was a Catholic, but quickly added: Catholic by fate, by birth, not by choice. I answered that therefore he was no longer Catholic because this opinion was the equivalent of a choice. He agreed, but replied: freedom consists in choosing our fate. So, then, he was Catholic by an accident of birth and by his free acceptance of that accident – in other words he brought two heresies into his religion. For him, moreover, Catholicism was less a doctrine and a set of rules than a tradition and a way of life. He neither accepted nor rejected the dogmas: he lived them, he endured them – especially when he transgressed. In morality as in aesthetics he loved the exception, the singularity. But exceptions are dependent on rules, and every violation renders homage to the norm. Was he aware of this contradiction? I don't know, but I can say that his best poems are a response to this conflict. A response and a resolution, in terms that are not moral but aesthetic and vital.

Villaurrutia's distrust of inspiration led him to distrust prolificacy as well. This is strange: his enemy was not fecundity but sterility. What's more, he knew it: he not only passed through long periods of aridity, but made them the subject of several of his best poems. In his critical essays, he occasionally alluded to his laziness; in his conversations with me he often spoke of it. In a poem that revealingly takes as its title a line from the *Inferno* – the words with which Francesca begins her story: *amor condusse noi ad una morte* – Xavier identifies love with this laziness which is then identified with death. The true name of this "indolence" is *acedia,* the sickness of the spirit described by theologians and doctors of the Middle Ages and the Renaissance. It is the disease of those who are contemplative and religious, the melancholy of Hamlet and of Dürer's angel, Ficino's bile or black humor, Baudelaire's *ennui.*

The demon of midday, who appears at the moment when the sun pauses for an instant in the center of the sky, was, according to the Church Fathers, the creature who inspired the visions of acedia. The medieval demon of midday was transformed into the romantic demon of midnight. Diurnal or nocturnal, the visions it instills are at once erotic and funereal; Nerval's melancholic *tenebreux* is the eternal widower: his love is a shadow and the constellation shining in his lute is disputed by Saturn and Isis. Possessed by images which are alternatingly lascivious and mournful, the victim of acedia falls into a stupor that is interrupted by spasms of rage and raptures of enthusiasm. Sufferers of melancholy are both irascible and imaginative. For these reasons, it is a mistake to confuse acedia, a disease of the spirit and of those who are spiritual, with simple laziness. Acedia paralyzes its victim and yet does not permit him a moment of rest. It is both stupor and anguish, a pride that petrifies us and an anxiety that forces us into ceaseless motion, an immobility broken by bursts of creative activity. The victim of acedia cannot touch the reality that is in front of him, but he can converse with ghosts and make stones speak.

My acquaintance with Xavier Villaurrutia did not change any of my ideas or introduce me to any new ones. He was indifferent to philosophy, morality, and politics, or too modest to discuss such matters at a café table; our conversations centered around a poem, a book, an author. I have always liked difficult poetry, poetry that has a secret; Villaurrutia showed me that in order to be secret, secrets must be shared. Sharing is not divulging, and the true art is not in obscurity but in chiaroscuro. I have always believed in inspiration: Villaurrutia helped me to distinguish it from facileness and to avoid confusing it with process. I have always been attracted to words, those double or triple creatures; Villaurrutia warned me to distrust them. A drop of doubt must be added to what we say; the shadow of incertitude must accompany our affirmations. Because of the nature of the Spanish language and the Spanish tradition, emphatic, categorical verse is the great temptation of our poets. Villaurrutia taught me to read poems with other eyes; or rather, he taught me that a poem is not read only with the eyes but with all the senses and the intellect. In addition to their meaning, words have weight, color, flavor, scent. Above all they have shadows and echoes: with them the poet shapes instantaneous sculptures.

VISIONS AND OVERSIGHTS

THOUGH VILLAURRUTIA'S LIFE was immersed in literature, his work is sparse, as if he had spent most of his time doing something besides writing. He was, above all else, a lyric poet, but his complete poems scarcely fill a slim volume of a hundred pages or so, only a tenth of his entire output. The rest consists of plays, criticism, and a number of texts which approach the novel or the short story without really being either. His plays make up half of his work in prose. He had a great enthusiasm for the theatre, and toward the end of his life it became his central occupation. While I admire his perseverance, his obstinacy surprises me. Was he really what is called a "man of the theatre"? The answer, of course, is no. His plays are well-crafted and intelligent, and some of them contain admirable passages, but they lack an essential element: theatricality. They are nonetheless of interest in one obvious way: as a social document. It is odd that those of our literary critics with sociological inclinations have not realized that whatever their literary merit may be, these plays are an exact though inadvertent portrait of the Mexican middle class during the second quarter of this century. I hasten to clarify: these plays are a document more for what they do not say than for what they say.

All of Villaurrutia's plays – short or long, comedies or dramas – are ruled by the same aesthetic. He took his inspiration from the French tradition: the great dramatists of the seventeenth century and certain of the moderns such as Giraudoux and Lenormand; he was, *hélas,* also influenced by the realist authors of the beginning of the century and the theatre of the *boulevard*. Strangely enough, he was either uninterested in the theatre of the avant-garde, or unable – or unwilling – to profit from its discoveries. He strove to observe the three unities – time, place, and action – and to move his characters within those limits. His plays are precisely constructed, but formulaic. His theatrical work is very correct, but if there are no blunders, neither are there innovations. The short plays are somewhat insubstantial, though undeniably well-written. Each character rivals the others in the art of uttering distinguished trivialities, and the conflicts are as vague and flimsy as the characters. One searches these plays in vain for the fantasy, sarcasm, verbal deliria, violence, and explosive humor of the Surrealist farces and short plays, or those written by Lorca and Alberti in Spain.

The plays in three acts are well-constructed but lack a theatrical dimension: they are to true theatre what a sketch is to an oil painting. The action is propelled not by ambition, power, or money, but by erotic desires that are almost always in conflict with social morality, that is, the family. Erotic passions and family ties constitute the double fatality of Villaurrutia's theatre. I don't know if I can call this fatality intelligent, but in any case it is *reasoning;* his characters think out loud, and, like their author, often take pleasure in hearing what they are thinking. It is a theatre of situations more than of characters. The passions never break free of all restraint and the conflicts dissipate before they are resolved. His two most ambitious plays are *Invitación a la muerte* [Invitation to Death] and *La hiedra* [The Ivy]–one inspired by *Hamlet,* the other by Racine. In both plays there are brilliant moments, ingenious retorts, intense monologues, dramatic situations. But it is the artistry of a wax museum. Not Racine but Moratín.

In his notes to the set designer, Villaurrutia insists on the "good taste" of the furniture and the decor. How could he have forgotten that today's good taste is inelegant tomorrow? The language that his characters speak now seems as remote as the furnishings of the rooms they move through, as dusty as the fatuous mirrors in which they catch sight of themselves. A psychological theatre without conflicts of class, generation, or ideas. The closed world of the families of the upper middle class which still preserved the French-style manners of the beginnings of the century. A world of papas and daughters, mamas and sons, sisters-in-law and brothers. In a corner, discreet maids incapable of committing an error of language or of tact. The sign that rules this hermetic society, this miniscule solar system, is the circle. Naturally and foreseeably, at some point in the dialogue–a ploy repeated on three or four occasions–a cynic will observe that the matter under discussion is a vicious circle. But not too vicious. The moral code of these families is the same as Villaurrutia's: decency, decorum, reserve. Modest forms of pride. The characters speak like the heroes of French comedies but their morality is traditional, Hispanic, criollo. The passions that torment them are those which menace the sanctity of the home and the integrity of the family: adultery and incest (though the latter is insinuated rather than stated outright). Allusions to other sexual inclinations are vague.

The moral axis around which the characters revolve and which is at the center of almost all the conflicts is *legitimacy.* It is no accident that one of these plays is entitled *La mujer legítima* [The Legitimate Wife], that the heroine of another was born out of wedlock, and that the *Hamlet*-like conflict of *Invitación a la muerte* takes place between a son, an adulterous mother, and a phantom father. Legitimacy is the great obsession of Mexican families. Of course, we are a nation where every self-respecting gentleman has a "little home" away from home. The tradition goes back to the colonial period. Everyone who has ever dealt with the parochial archives of the seventeenth and eighteenth centuries has noticed the frequent mention of "child of the Church," a euphemism for bastard. The custom has not fallen into disuse and in Mexico, as in the rest of Hispanic America, the proportion of children born out of wedlock is one of the highest in the world. It is another of the premodern traits of our country.

Neither our literary critics nor our sociologists have paused to consider the parallel: legitimacy is also the secret theme of the history of Mexico from the moment of its independence. Or rather, from the moment when México-Tenochtitlán was founded. Both Aztec society and the society of New Spain sought the consecration of legitimacy. The Aztec rulers were painfully conscious of their status as usurpers or illegitimate heirs, and governed in the name of the true proprietors and kings of the earth, the legendary Toltecs; they considered themselves, as Moctezuma told Cortés, "their substitutes." The same questioning of the legitimacy of their domination troubled the Spaniards and gave rise to the disputes over the legality of the conquest and the doctrines of the evangelizing mission of the Spanish monarchy. Republican Mexico has also experienced these doubts. The profound meaning of the ritual of September 15, the *Grito* [Shout], would be lost on us if we failed to realize that the ceremony is a dual one: on the one hand, it is a symbolic resurrection of the Mexican nation, and on the other, a consecration of its legitimate authority. More than a democratic celebration it is a political liturgy impregnated with religiousness.

Villaurrutia was unaware of the historical ramifications of the subject and dealt with it from a point of view that was strictly traditional and psychological. His tableau suffers from unreality. He describes an archetype that had lost all its vigor. At the end of the century, during the period of their fascination with Paris, the old criollo families had accepted it, but the Revolution and the influence of North America swept away the French model. By the time Villaurrutia was writing, the Mexican bourgeoisie was no longer like that; its manners and ideals were not those described in his plays. The Mexican family was and is louder and more vulgar, more avid and sensual, vital and imaginative. There isn't a person among us who speaks like the characters of *La hiedra* or *Parece mentira* [It Seems Unbelievable]; no one uses "alterca-tion" to say "fight." Our language isn't that correct; it is also richer and more energetic. Ultimately, Villaurrutia closed his eyes to the gro-tesque, absurd, or fantastic aspects of reality and constructed a theatre without claws and without wings, a theatre which was neither realism nor imagination, neither criticism nor poetry. His characters are rea-sonable and reasoning shadows who never for a moment become aware of their own unreality. Ghosts who never knew they were ghosts.

Villaurrutia — one of the most intelligent and lucid Mexicans of the first half of this century, admirer of Gide's *L'immoraliste* and translator of Blake's *The Marriage of Heaven and Hell,* a man who was not afraid to expose his erotic inclinations to a society dominated by a ferocious and obtuse machismo, a poet at once deep and sublime — didn't see or didn't want to see the world in which he lived. He didn't want to see himself within that world. For the reality of Mexico — brutal, sordid, colorful: alive — he substituted an unreality that was mediocre and, worse, gray. Blindness? More probably: conformity. Villaurrutia's characters may violate social laws but they never question the validity of those laws. Criticism, in the moral and philosophical sense of the word, is a notion that is entirely foreign to them. Useless to remind them of another word: *rebellion*. It would have burned their lips. None-theless, Villaurrutia was, in his own way, a rebel. His blindness — we will call it that — was shared by his entire generation, even Novo can-not be excluded from it. Not until Carlos Fuentes's *Where the Air is Clear* did the characteristics and the language of the Mexican bourgeoi-sie finally appear in our literature.

VILLAURRUTIA'S CRITICISM takes up about the same amount of space in his *Complete Works* as the plays. As a critic, Xavier was unri-valed: he had a sure eye, an acute ear, and a mind that was both pene-trating and receptive. In the practice of criticism, however, innate tal-ent, great as it may be, is not enough; culture is also required. Frequent contact with artistic and literary works not only refines us but also changes us to a point where we begin to acquire a second nature. There is a critical instinct, an instinct that is not natural but that can merge with our feelings and become natural. This instinct is called taste, and it is at once the foundation and the limit of criticism: the foundation, because without taste, without an affective relationship to the work, the aesthetic experience cannot be realized; the limit, because every work of art that matters always transcends the taste of its time. Taste both reveals works of art to us and obscures them. Xavier's taste was almost infallible, but he knew that great art is that which goes beyond taste.

In addition to taste, criticism requires imagination. The function of criticism consists, first, in separating and dissociating the disparate elements that make up the work. Next, these elements must be associated, seen in relation to each other and to other works. During this second step, the imagination – the analogizing faculty which associates, compares and discovers hidden correspondences and significant oppositions – intervenes. Xavier was a poet and had a highly developed faculty of critical imagination. Finally, criticism demands selflessness, and Villaurrutia's best critical texts are exemplary in their generosity and spiritual sympathy.

Xavier's literary erudition, especially regarding poetry, was wide-ranging and profound. His knowledge of the plastic arts was more limited, as he lacked any experience of the great museums of Europe. Nevertheless, reproductions, books, and contact with Mexican painters and their works partly made up for this deficiency. He was not an essayist in the strict sense of the word, I mean, in the sense in which Alfonso Reyes, author of unsystematic texts on every imaginable subject, was a great essayist. However, he was an essayist in the sense that Eliot, W.H. Auden or Jean Paulhan were essayists: unsystematic critics of literary and pictorial works of art. Like those of Ortega y Gasset or Valéry, Reyes's best essays are works of imagination; Villaurrutia's essays, luminous as they might seem to us, depend on the work they analyze. With Villaurrutia, essentially a poet, criticism dismantles imaginative works; with Reyes, essentially an essayist, criticism constructs texts which, in their own way, are also works of the imagination.

In one of his first articles, on Antonio Caso's *Principios de estética* [Principles of Aesthetics], he makes a distinction between "Aesthetics written with a capital 'A' and aesthetics written without one." The former is that of philosophers and professors, "who consider it a science worthy to stand beside Logic and Ethics." The latter is that of artists, poets, and critics, "a personal æsthetics, fabricated out of various readings . . . and shaped by limitations, elective affinities, simple prejudices." It is an exact definition. Philosophers often forget that works of art are not illustrations of theories but vice versa. Villaurrutia's distrust of systems was not due to ignorance or to the anti-intellectualism from which artists and poets sometimes suffer. His article on Caso reveals that he knew the work of Croce, Bergson, Meumann, and Fechner, and that he was acquainted – whether directly or through Caso I don't know – with the doctrines of Kant, Schelling, and Hegel concerning art. His reading of Croce's book on "the dead and the living in Hegel's philosophy" was probably his initial exposure to Croce's thought, as had been the case with André Breton shortly before. In any case, unlike Breton, he was not particularly influenced by the book, nor did it incite him to probe more deeply into Hegelianism or Marxism. His literary and artistic judgment manifests various affinities and differences, but these do not correspond to any predetermined intellectual system.

His frequent contact with the poets and writers of our language, Spaniards and Latin Americans as well as Mexicans, began in his early youth. His reading of French literature also began when he was very young; it never ended, and marked him profoundly. He later became acquainted with British and North American literature. I don't know when he began to read Dante, but I do know that he often cited Dante in conversation. One trait separated him from the other members of his generation, an affinity for modern Italian literature, especially the prose writers, from Pirandello to Bontempelli. The map of his literary preferences displays the extent and also the coherence of his tastes. To begin with, in the Baroque period, he was closer to Quevedo than to Góngora, and closer to Sor Juana than to Quevedo. Later, guided by Eliot, he discovered the English metaphysical poets. Influenced by Gide, he translated Blake, and it was a memorable translation. Another permanent passion was French Symbolism. From Albert Beguin's book on German Romanticism, he learned a different way of reading Nerval and the Surrealists. He was also a great reader of the *modernistas* and their heirs; he was especially drawn to three poets: Lugones, Juan Ramón Jiménez, and, of course, López Velarde. Affinities: in Spain, with Jorge Guillén, Gerardo Diego, Marichalar, and Jarnés Millán; in Cuba, with Jorge Mañach; in Argentina, with Borges, Francisco Luis

Bernárdez and Enrique Molinari. (I'm not forgetting Luis Cardoza y Aragón, but he is really Mexican as well as Guatemalan.)

The French influence on his literary and moral evolution was decisive: he was dazzled by Cocteau, liberated and justified by Gide. Another influence no less profound than Gide's but limited to the realm of aesthetic ideas was that of Valéry. Other French readings and predilections included Giraudoux and Paul Morand. In the English language he was impressed by Eliot, of course, and by George Santayana. All of these essayists contributed to the elaboration of his poetics, which was a kind of pact between his Classicist inclinations and his Romantic impulses. It is no accident that he considered Baudelaire the principal figure of the modern tradition, since Baudelaire is the point of convergence between Romanticism and Classicism.

The amount of space the critical texts take up in his *Complete Works* is deceptive. In reality, Xavier wrote only a few essays; the rest are brief articles written for pay. But his half-dozen essays count among the best works of modern Mexican criticism. The most well-known and esteemed of his essays, and rightly so, is his study of López Velarde. Faithful to his ideal of what a critic should be – when the critic is a poet – Villaurrutia acknowledged that "when I tried to explain Ramón López Velarde's spritual complexity, I did nothing more than help myself discover and examine my own drama. It has been said that the novel is an autobiographical genre; it appears reasonable to me to think that, in the same way, criticism is always a form of self-criticism." Little can be added to this declaration of principles, which is also a confession.

More than a discovery, Villaurrutia's essay was a resurrection: López Velarde lay buried under the tombstone of an obtuse admiration. By bringing him back into the light, Xavier showed us that he was not an embalmed cadaver but a living poet. Whom does Villaurrutia's López Velarde most resemble, Villaurrutia himself or the real López Velarde? Unquestionably he resembles Villaurrutia, because both of them resemble Baudelaire. They are his descendants. All three poets are children of the sun. Not of Rimbaud's sun, but of the blackened sun of Melancholy, the midday demon's sun which also belongs to the ghosts of midnight. Villaurrutia revealed to us the true spiritual genealogy of a poet whom provincial Mexican criticism had insisted on considering a provincial.

Xavier's other literary essays are more or less marginal. They do not discover new authors or unknown aspects of a known work; neither do they found a tradition. The prologue to *Laurel* reveals his strong points and his weaknesses; though his gaze was sure and he touched on all the essentials, he went only halfway. He was not a miner. Nor was he an explorer; he was not attracted by limits or by the limitless. His criticism lacks perspective, it has no horizons. There are several texts – I am thinking especially of the short articles and, among them, of those written in his youth – which escape from these limitations. For example, his portraits of Francisco A. de Icaza ("He was not influential; he was, however, exemplary"), Salvador Novo ("A young man in the big city; it was the time of long sentences and short pants"), Efrén Hernández ("Builder of castles in the air"), Luis Cardoza y Aragón ("Somnambulant Sagittarius shooting off a rain of arrows that hit undreamed-of targets"). The true critic not only sees better than others do, more clearly and more deeply, but also has the gift of foresight. Criticism is vision and prophecy. Villaurrutia could see, and could foresee. For example, several days ago, a young graduate student had me reread an article Xavier wrote in 1925, on José Gorostiza's *Canciones para cantar en las barcas* [Songs to Sing in Boats]. In a few short phrases, Xavier anticipated the theme of what would become one of the great modern poems of our language, *Muerte sin fin* [Death without End]: glass and water. The lines in which he refers to Gorostiza's poetry, comparing it to water, are worth citing: "Better than the apparent purity of a spring's water, into which any hand can dip, his thin stream of water runs directly from the filter into the harmonious geometry of the glass. And how often the glass's transparent solidity becomes indistinguishable from its contents."

Among the longer essays is one which deserves to be singled out: "Introducción a la poesía mexicana" [Introduction to Mexican Poetry]. This text confirms, once more, that "criticism is a form of auto-criticism." The general idea comes from Reyes, Pedro Henríquez Ureña, and Castro Leal: Mexican poetry has "a tone of intimacy, a tone of confession"; our poetry is reflective and meditative; its color is "pearl gray"; its hour, twilight. This idea has been refuted several times and I myself, in 1942 (while Xavier was still alive), wrote a small essay demonstrating that this vision did violence to the reality of our poetry. But Xavier's essay is attractive for its quality of self-description. His poetry is indeed remote, solitary, intimate, aristocratic. It is also reflective, in the physical as well as the psychological sense: it is a precise and precious construction of reflections, a poetry that loves form, and that has the restrained luminosity of an opal.

Among the distinctive traits of Mexican poetry Xavier mentions is continuity. It is a characteristic he shares with other Mexican poets. His poetry, and he knew this well, inserts itself into a tradition, the same tradition to which Sor Juana and Manuel José Othón, Enrique González Martínez and José Juan Tablada, Amado Nervo and Carlos Pellicer belonged. Like all traditions, it is made up of ruptures which become links. Awareness of this continuity was strong in Xavier's generation and in mine as well, an awareness that did not prevent us from feeling ourselves to be part of the modern Western tradition. I believe this was (and is) the attitude of the generation that came after us, but I wonder if the youngest poets feel the same. If they don't, it would be an ominous sign: it would mean that Mexico's identity was cracking. To repeat what I wrote years ago: "Rebellion against tradition doesn't trouble me; what worries me is the absence of tradition."

Xavier's writings on theater seem to me to be less modern and less stimulating than his ideas about poetry. However, many of the texts on the plastic arts are excellent. I will single out the one on Rufino Tamayo, the first study of any importance done on him. Tamayo's art was not very close to Xavier's sensibility; nevertheless, he understood and admired the simplicity of its construction and its boldness of color. In a brief note on the photographer Manuel Alvarez Bravo, he made the acute comment that "like St. Dionysius, [Alvarez Bravo] has his head in the right place, since he has it in his hands." His favorite painters were Julio Castellanos and Agustín Lazo, the latter a close friend with whom he collaborated in his theatrical endeavors. The texts on Lazo are intelligent and sharp, like Lazo himself.

Among his art criticism is a text that was very famous in its time: "José Clemente Orozco and Horror." It seems to me to be an example of incomprehension. Didactic, sarcastic, pathetic, Orozco's painting deserves, in its moments of greatest intensity, to be called terrible: it impresses us, it takes us by suprise. But horror is something very different. Horror is paralyzing dread, a contradictory fixation – awe and fascination are mingled with fear, disgust, and nausea – a complex feeling that is very close to the experience of the sacred.[1] In Orozco's work there is terror, not horror. In place of the lines from Baudelaire he cites, Xavier could have remembered these, which express what horror really is with great lucidity:

> Sleep itself is an enormous lair,
> Filled with vague horror, leading none knows where;
> All windows open upon Infinity;
>
> My spirit, always haunted now by slumber,
> Yearns for extinction, insensibility...[2]

The opposition between terror and horror is of the same order as that between the active and the passive, the erect and the prone, fear and fascination. Baudelaire says that his spirit has been bewitched by vertigo. Horror is a vertigo, a dizziness: we feel a wave of nausea and we collapse. Horror is a fall, in the theological sense of the word. It is born from surprise, it is an amazement at something – being or object – that frightens us. One of the ingredients of horror is the unheard-of, the never before seen. Horror immobilizes us because it is made of contradictory feelings: fear and seduction, repulsion and attraction. Horror is a fascination. The object that fills us with horror is not necessarily menacing or dangerous, as it must be in the case of terror. The terrible, that which causes dread and terror, is actively harmful and severe. Jupiter's thunderbolt, Jehovah's wrath, Kali's sword are all terrible, not horrible. Tamerlane is also terrible, as are earthquakes, wildfires, Hitler, an epidemic, Stalin. In terror there is agression, not fascination. Terror is an accumulation of power suddenly unleashed, destroying everything it touches; terror manifests itself by attacking; the

[1] I have dealt with the subject in *The Bow and the Lyre* in the chapter titled "The Other Shore," and in an untranslated essay titled "Risa y penitencia," collected in *Puertas al campo*.

[2] Trans. Jackson Matthews, in M. & J. Matthews ed., Baudelaire, *The Flowers of Evil*.

natural reaction to it is flight or, if we have the strength and the spirit, resistance. Horror does not attack; it as a presence that paralyzes us; in the wake of this paralysis come vertigo and fascination; horror is a magnet. But I am being inexact in speaking of presence; horror is a presence which reveals itself as an absence. It is the obverse of being. That is why Baudelaire speaks of a "large hole." Terror is phallic and agressive; it is the One, the Chief, God the Father, just or vengeful, always implacable. Horror is immobility, the great yawn of empty space, the womb and the hole in the earth, the universal Mother and the great garbage heap, the Zero and its double face: birth and annihilation. With horror, we cannot have recourse to flight or combat; there remains only adoration or exorcism.

Another essay, "Pintura sin mancha" [Unstained painting] is memorable both for its form and for its felicitous exploration of the relationships between painting and poetry. Villaurrutia asks that "painters make their paintings more poetical as I have tried to give my poetry more plasticity." The ultimate correspondence of painting and poetry cannot be arrived at by the abolition of their differences; it must be reached through those very differences: "If the aim of poetry is to make us think of the unthinkable, perhaps the object of painting is none other than making visible the invisible . . . To make visible the invisible! . . . A magical operation, a religious operation, a poetic operation." And he concludes: "The common denominator of the arts is poetry."

This affirmation can be extended to his prose which, more than once, approaches poetry. Approaches, but never confuses itself with poetry. At the opposite extreme from Novo's prose, Villaurrutia's is neither colloquial nor idiomatic. His ideal is not naturalness but geometry: the fluidity of his use of language is not the fluidity of a brook but that of water flowing through strict channels. Sobriety and exactness in the adjectives, a wise combination of abstract concepts and concrete and material expressions, a calm and spacious rhythm, a prose that moves in surges and endeavors simultaneously to seduce and to convince. Villaurrutia is one of our greatest writers of prose, but for all its purity and flawlessness, his prose is not Spanish – it is French. Baudelaire was his model. From the French poet, he learned the secret of the sinuous and volatile sentence that seems to reflect and turn back on itself only to move forward, and that reveals in its meanderings an unknown landscape. A sentence unwinding in spirals ending in a sudden illumination. Prose like a bend in a river, that doubles back for a phrase or two, contemplates itself for an instant, and goes on. Prose that is not like a mirror but like a consciousness, exploring the world and itself.

THE SLEEPER AWAKE

VILLAURRUTIA'S FIRST POEMS began appearing in magazines in 1919, when he was barely sixteen years old. Spanish *modernismo* was on its last legs, and Vicente Huidobro had already published *Ecuatorial* [Equatorial], *Poemas árticos* [Arctic Poems] and *El espejo de agua* [The Mirror of Water]. In Mexico, López Velarde's *Zozobra* [Disquiet] and Tablada's *Un día...* [One Day...] were published that same year. But the adolescent Xavier was still under the spell of the *modernistas*. His masters were Lugones, González Martínez, Juan Ramón Jiménez, and Amado Nervo. He also read the French Symbolists and there is more than an echo, in his earliest poems, of Rodenbach and Albert Samain (one of whose poems he translated for the magazine *Ateneo de Honduras* [Atheneum of Honduras] in 1923). Villaurrutia evolved very quickly and by the end of this period he was already writing poems under the double influence of López Velarde and Francis Jammes. Although the poems from this time are exercises or imitations, they reveal various qualities that persist in his later poetry: a sharp and sensitive ear for the cadence of the line and the play of accents and syllables; a precise and flexible syntax; an imagination of such plasticity that every poem, every strophe is a small universe of verbal and even visual relationships; and an instinctive awareness of limits, of "how far to go," so that even in these youthful poems there are neither sentimental excesses nor intellectual contortions. In short, a consciousness of form unusual in a poet so young, coupled with a sensibility that was more intense than extensive, more finely-tuned than powerful.

Reflejos [Reflections] was published in 1926. It was his first book. Those were the years of the avant-garde, but Xavier was singularly timid about the new style and adopted from it only the negations: *no* to sentimental confession and anecdote, reduction of the poem to its essential lines, hatred of amplifications, preeminence of sight over hearing, preference for assonant rhyme and blank verse. There are echoes of López Velarde and especially of the Juan Ramón Jiménez of *Eternidades* [Eternities] and *Piedra y cielo* [Stone and Sky]. The resemblance of certain of these poems to others written in the same period by various Spanish and South American poets is simply due to the fact that those poets, like Villaurrutia, were studying Jiménez. Although Juan Ramón's influence is deplored today, I think it was beneficial: if it was not the poetic purity it was believed to be at the time, it was a rhetorical purification. Spanish poetry was stripped bare of its corsets and fripperies and, unburdened, began moving forward. There are other influences and affinities in *Reflejos:* "Suite del insomnio" [The Insomniac's Suite] reveals an attentive reading of Tablada and there are echoes of Carlos Pellicer in "Aire y Cezanne." In every case, Villaurrutia transforms whatever influenced him and writes very personal poems, poems only he could have written. He transmutes Jiménez's vague poetry into a precise construction, airy and somewhat dry; he turns Pellicer's *fauvism* into a geometry; he infuses Tablada's *haikai* with severity and gravity. Some of the poems in this book — "Cuadro" [Painting], "Amplificaciones," "Suite del insomnio" — prefigure the later work. One poem, "Solo, sin soledad" [Alone, without loneliness], contains the punning wordplay that would become one of the distinctive traits of the mature poetry, as well as the synesthetic games in which disturbing geometries are constructed out of echoes:

> The night plays with noises
> copying them in its mirrors
> of sounds.[1]

It is no accident that "Suite del insomnio" is the last poem in *Reflejos*. In 1929, "Nocturno de la estatua" [Nocturne: The Statue] is published in the magazine *Contemporáneos*. With this poem, insomnia peers

---

[1] *La noche juega con los ruidos*
copiándolos en sus espejos
de sonidos.

down into the well of dreams and begins convening its ghostly popula-
tion. Other Nocturnes followed this first one until 1933, when Villaur-
rutia publishes a *plaquette* with ten Nocturnes, under the poet-printer
Miguel N. Lira's Fabula imprint. This is the nucleus of his most impor-
tant book, *Nostalgia for Death* (1938). In 1941, various uncollected
poems, among them "Décima muerte" [Death in Décimas], are gath-
ered into another small volume. All of these poems except one titled
"Poesía" [Poetry] were united in the second and definitive edition of
Nostalgia for Death (1946).

Nostalgia for Death (1946) is divided into three parts: "Nocturnes,"
"Other Nocturnes," and "Nostalgias." The poems in first part are in
the same order as in the 1933 *plaquette* except that one poem, "Noc-
turno miedo" [Nocturne: Fear], has been added. The other poems in
this section represent the moment when Villaurrutia most decisively
embraces the aesthetics of the avant-garde, and even ventures into the
outskirts of Surrealism. "Nocturne: Fear," however, is reminiscent,
even in meter, of Rubén Darío's three "Nocturnos." It is not inferior
to the other poems, it is simply different. To be precise: it is different
not in its subject matter, but in its construction and its verbal material.
In the second part, "Other Nocturnes," as well, some poems such as
"Nocturno," "Cuando la tarde . . . " [When Evening . . .] and "Estan-
cias nocturnas" [Nocturnal Stanzas] which did not appear in the 1938
edition of *Nostalgia for Death,* were added. In the first of these poems
Darío's voice is visible – or, rather, audible – and in the last part of the
third, as Alí Chumacero points out, José Asunción Silva's voice can be
detected. In spite of these differences and disharmonies, the unity of
Nostalgia for Death is admirable: a unity of inspiration, tone, and color.
The title strikes me as infelicitous: the *jeu d'esprit* is forced and a bit too
clever. But one of the essential books of modern poetry has an even
more unfortunate title: *Les fleurs du mal*.

The first part of *Nostalgia for Death,* with the exception of the late ad-
dition "Nocturne: Fear," contains Xavier's most daring poems. He
had made a double discovery: of his subject and of modern poetry. I
don't believe that his subject was death, at least not exclusively. I don't
believe it, even though he says it and the title of his book declares it to
be so, because in these poems death is intimately linked to sleep, and
both are linked to the night. The identification of sleep with death is

one of the oldest commonplaces of Western poetry. At the same time, and especially since Romanticism, sleep has been identified with life; sleep is not death but the other aspect of life. Sleep is dreams: the forms – absurd and monstrous in appearance but impregnated with meaning – by which life manifests itself. With psychoanalysis, sleep ceases to be Quevedo's "mute image of death" and becomes the hieroglyphic writing of desire. Certainly, among the signs traced by desire, death occupies a central place. Eroticism and death are as inseparable a pair as day and night, waking and sleep. Romanticism's originality lay in its attempt to dissolve, in the great night of origin, the opposition between love and death in a unity that precedes consciousness and human existence itself. In one of his *Hymns to the Night,* Novalis alludes explicitly to the "desire for death" as an amorous desire. But his death is not a fall into a dreamless sleep like pagan death; rather, it is return to a state that does not even require the abolition of the body. A poetry that is literally eucharistic:

> One day everything will be a body
> A single body
> And the blessed couple
> Will bathe in that celestial blood

With a magnificent violence that mingles exasperation and despair, Surrealism brings together the Romantic vision and the discoveries of psychoanalysis. There is a very real and, for that reason, fertile contradiction here: Surrealist oneirism merges prophecy and obsession, clairvoyance and psychic disturbance, Novalis and Freud.

In Xavier Villaurrutia's case, the revelation of the poetry of sleep was linked to the discovery of Surrealism and of other modern poets more or less influenced by oneirism. But Villaurrutia's early poetry, as we have seen, conformed to a poetics of lucidity: the poet is not simply listening to the dictations of the unconscious, he is guiding the unconscious murmur, imposing a form on it and transforming it into an intelligible language. This conflict is the true subject of the Nocturnes, whose poetry is inhabited by a double opposition: sleep and waking, consciousness and delirium. The epigraph from the Elizabethan poet Michael Drayton defines this contradiction: "Burn'd in a sea of yce and drown'd amidst a fire." The contradiction is existential and verbal, vital and rhetorical. I mean: the poetic drama consists in this opposition and from it emerges the tension of the language. I wrote "poetic drama" because this is the conflict that appears in his poems. I don't know if it corresponds to a "real drama." To understand the poems it is enough to know that it functions as if it were indeed real.

Villaurrutia was fully conscious of the duality within him. In a letter to Bernardo Ortiz de Montellano he says, "The poet's subject is sleep . . . but it is a very difficult subject to address. Either you treat it as the Surrealists have . . . or else as a poetic subject invented or reinvented by the lucid, wakeful poet." His temperament and instincts inclined him towards the second tactic: "Only the hand of someone who is wide awake can write the poem of sleep." At the end of the prologue to the *Laurel* anthology, in a recapitulation of his generation's poetry that is also an examination of his own, he points out that what distinguishes these poets "is the current of irrationality, derived from French poetic movements . . ." But if the work of certain poets "seems to develop out of the purest abandon, that of others, and with greater intensity, develops out of the most profound attention." The latter attitude – he says it without saying it – is his: "It should be kept in mind that, though they have not disdained the current of irrationalism but have, on the contrary, assimilated the new possibilities and contributions of this form of freedom, other spirits remain – even while sleeping – awake, in a state of constant wakefulness."

In another text written a little later, but which sums up his ideas very well, he says "Never except in German Romanticism, never except now in modern and contemporary poetry which so naturally attaches itself to true Romanticism and which seems to prolong and perpetuate it in a thousand obvious or obscure, open or secret ways, have the relationships between waking and sleep been closer or more profound." This declaration appears in the essay on Nerval (1942) and can be seen as a reversal of the opinions he held fifteen years earlier. At the same time, this change retrospectively articulates the sense of his poetic project between 1927 and 1937, the ten years during which he wrote what was at once the richest and the strictest part of his poetic work – the poems collected in the 1938 edition of *Nostalgia for Death*. It is significant that Villaurrutia does not formulate the poetics that justifies his practice between 1927 and 1937 until 1942. "The poem," Unamuno said, "is a postceptual thing, while dogma is a preceptual thing."

The revelation of sleep is inseparable, for Villaurrutia, from the discovery of modern poetry. The forms of the ten initial poems of *Nostalgia for Death* (1938) reflect the diversity of paths and temptations. A diversity, it must be repeated, which does not compromise the unity of tone or inspiration. Only three poems are written in free verse and in one of them, "Nocturno eterno" [Nocturne: The Eternal], lines of eleven and fourteen syllables abound. The rest consists of two *décimas* (stanzas of ten octosyllabic lines), one poem in assonant octosyllables and four in blank verse. The final poem is a sonnet in unrhymed alexandrines. The *décimas* exchange gestures of recognition with Guillén and Valéry, though no one would confuse them with poems by those two poets. As he gave himself over to the flow of the unconscious, Villaurrutia was ever mindful of Valéry's "wakefulness." This attitude brought him close to the other French poet who is also present in the first Nocturnes: Jules Supervielle. The adversarial couplings of sleep/wakefulness, ice/flames, time/eternity, and others like them, which are the center of Villaurrutia's poetic system, also appear in Supervielle. One of his most beautiful books, which Xavier must have read and re-read, is called *Le Forçat Innocent* [The Innocent Convict]. The names of Valéry and Supervielle immediately summon up that of Cocteau. He was much read and much admired by Xavier, who drew certain of his subjects – roses, angels – from Cocteau, but it seems to me that Cocteau's influence manifested itself more in Xavier's mannerisms and defiances than in his poetry.

In the first Nocturnes appear objects, beings, and materials – statues, shadows, walls, mirrors, marble, smoke, corners, stairways, deserted streets – that bring to mind not a poet but a painter: de Chirico. The name de Chirico brings us back to sleep and Surrealism. In de Chirico, there is no pictorial automatism; there is instead a vision in which different realities and different times are juxtaposed, confront each other, and coexist. This is the atmosphere Villaurrutia evokes at times in the Nocturnes. A "voice, lost, wandering the streets setting fires," a statue that stands up and cries out without crying out, a sky that is a floor that is a mirror that replicates words instead of bodies. All of it has, as in de Chirico's painting, an almost mineral solidity, and, at the same time, the consistency of a dream. Every poem is a sketch of precise lines that evoke confused and ambiguous states of being:

> In the middle of a silence deserted as a street before a crime
> not even breathing so that nothing will disturb my dying
> in this loneliness with no walls
> at this hour when angles are escaping
> I leave my bloodless statue in the tomb of my bed

It was natural that a poetics of this kind would find, in punning, a precise instrument. Villaurrutia confided to Ortiz de Montellano in the same letter: "Will you believe me if I tell you that not one unmotivated or gratuitous pun can be found in any of my poems? I don't use puns for play, I use them out of an inescapable necessity... I play with fire and run the risk of burning myself." Punning has been and is used in the poetry of all ages and all languages. Undoubtedly Villaurrutia was inspired by the example of modern French poetry, though certain of his puns, such as the "afrentarán mi frente" of "Nocturno muerto" [Nocturne: The Dead] also appear in the work of Lope de Vega. From the start, the surrealists were attracted to puns: one need only remember the name of Rrose Sélavy, associated with Marcel Duchamp but also with Robert Desnos, purveyor of phonetic and semantic marvels. There is a poem by Paul Eluard, dedicated, naturally, to de Chirico, which undoubtedly made a great impression on Villaurrutia and which can easily be seen as a prefiguration of the Nocturnes. The poem belongs to the book with the hispanicized title *Mourir de ne pas mourir* [To die of not dying] (1924), in which appears another poem ("L'amoureuse"), that Xavier translated years later.

GIORGIO DE CHIRICO

A wall denounces another wall
And the shadow protects me from my timid shadow
O tower of my love around my love,
All the white walls fled white around my silence.[2]

---

[2] *Un mur dénoce un autre mur*
Et l'ombre me défend de mon ombre peureuse.
O tour de mon amour autour de mon amour
Tous les murs filaient blanc autour de mon silence.
No translator credited; in Marcel Jean ed., *The Autobiography of Surrealism.*

The unquestionable affinities between modern French poetry and certain of the poems written by Villaurrutia during this period gave rise to a charge of plagiarism. Twenty-five years ago, I remember, it was still common to hear café-table critics – with vengeful eye and voice convulsed in resentment – recite a poem by Supervielle to condemn the despicable Villaurrutia. The poem is the first in a series titled "Saisir" [Seize] and belongs to *Le Forçat Innocent*. The resemblance between this poem and "Nocturne: The Statue" is undeniable, especially in the first lines, but the development and the conclusion could not be more different. Once again Villaurrutia takes his inspiration from someone else's poem and makes it his own. Supervielle's poem, in rhymed alexandrines, has ten lines; in the fifth and sixth, we witness a metamorphosis: the objects touched by the hand of the poet become birds; in turn, these birds return to their point of departure and convert themselves back into what they were: streets, shadows, walls, apples, statues. The poem presents us with a change that turns out to be a non-change, a return to the original situation:

SEIZE

Seize, seize the apple and the statue and the night,
Seize the shadow and the wall and the end of the street.

Seize the foot, the neck of the lady in bed
Then open your hands. How many birds released,

How many lost birds that turn into the street,
The shadow, the wall, the apple, the statue and the night?

Hands, you will wear yourselves out
At this dangerous game.

You will have to be cut
Off, one day, at the wrist.[3]

---

[3] Translated by James Kirkup. From *Jules Supervielle Selected Writings* (New York: New Directions, 1967).

Xavier's poem has thirteen lines of unrhymed free verse, and after the third line the similarity to Supervielle's poem begins to fade until it vanishes altogether in the following lines. The elements of Villaurrutia's poem are very different, even opposite—"chips" instead of birds—and its general movement consists in a metamorphosis that reveals itself to be a condemnation: the statue awakens only to say that it is "dying of sleep." Supervielle's is a poem of twilight. Villaurrutia's is nocturnal. I could enumerate other oppositions, but I believe that a reading of the poem in its entirety will amply confirm Xavier's originality and spare me a tedious substantiation of it.

The second section of *Nostalgia for Death* contains what are probably Villaurrutia's best poems. The form is more spacious, the language more direct, and the punning no longer as prominent. The line has an almost conversational rhythm, perhaps as a result of a reading of Eliot's famous essay on "music in poetry." "Nocturno en que habla la muerte" [Nocturne: Death Speaks], "Nocturno de los ángeles" [L. A. Nocturne: The Angels] (one of Villaurrutia's most erotic poems), "Nocturno rosa" [Nocturne: The Rose] and "Nocturno mar" [Nocturne: The Sea] represent the maturity, the highest moment of his poetry. There are two poems—both excellent—which belong to another period: "Nocturne" and "Nocturnal Stanzas." To me, these poems, like "Nocturne: Fear," in meter as well as in vocabulary and imagery, are a harkening back to the symbolist tradition and, more concretely, to the Darío of the "Nocturnos." There is also a distant and momentary affinity, faint, barely insinuated, with certain poems by Borges.

The third part, "Nostalgias," continues in the direction and the tone of the poems in the first two sections, but does not surpass them. The only novelty—except for "North Carolina Blues," a poem that is enchanting but incidental and accidental—is "Death in Décimas." Ten strict *décimas:* a sonorous and conceptual mechanism that is part toy, part syllogism, and part musical instrument. Certain readers have judged it his best poem. I disagree. I do admire its construction; the play of antitheses and paradoxes surprises me and makes me want to applaud at the close of each *décima*. The poem is a dramatic monologue and could have been written by a disciple of Calderón. It is the Spanish rhetoric of death, and it inspires in me neither the shudder of "Nocturno en que nada se oye" [Nocturne: Nothing Is Heard] nor the full and profound adherence of "Nocturne: Death Speaks."

His third and final book was *Canto a la primavera y otros poemas* (1948). There is a manifest decline: the form is less rigorous and the poetic vision is easier and more superficial. A return to classicism? No: a return to sentimental Romanticism. But some of the poems in this book continue in the direction initiated by "Nocturne: Fear," "Nocturne," and "Nocturnal Stanzas." Among them are several that can be counted among Xavier's best poems, such as "Amor condusse noi ad una morte," "Soneto de la Granada" [Sonnet of Granada], and "Madrigal sombrío" [Dark Madrigal]. Alí Chumacero notes that a poem by Novo, "Amor" [Love], is the direct antecedent of "Amor condusse noi ad una morte." This is correct, but it should be added that Novo's poem is purely lyrical, while Villaurrutia's is more spacious and complex, with a poetic density, a moral complexity, and human resonances that definitively set it apart from Novo's. These poems renew the ties to a tradition that allied formal perfection with the bitterness of age and the horror of existence. Poems that respond, without ever fully responding, to two questions, two doubts: who are we and where are we. It is fitting that the work of a man like Xavier, who was always surprised by the prodigious and simple fact of being alive, should end with this double interrogation. These questions are also a definition. Xavier belongs to the class of poets and of men we need most today: those who neither affirm nor negate, but who doubt and question themselves.

THE INFLUENCE of Rilke has often been discussed. Villaurrutia himself brought up Rilke's name in a conversation with José Luis Martínez (*Tierra Nueva*, March-April, 1940). He became acquainted with Rilke's work through its French translations, especially those by Maurice Betz. He says he was particularly impressed with *The Notebooks of Malte Laurids Brigge* and *Letters to a Young Poet,* though he confesses that the *Duino Elegies* and the *Sonnets to Orpheus* left him cold. The truth is that Villaurrutia's temperament was very different from Rilke's. The idea of "one's own death" is almost certainly drawn from the German poet's work, but Rilke's concept of death is very different from Villaurrutia's. For Xavier – Latin, Catholic, Mexican – death was not a pretext for flights into the metaphysical but a motivation for withdrawal and acceptance. Despite his love of French literature, he belonged to the Hispanic tradition, at once stoic and Christian: death is the end of this life and, for Christians, the leap into the other, eternal life. Rilke, the heir of Romanticism and Symbolism, confronts death not to accept it like a stoic or transcend it like a Christian – he confronts death to transform it. Death is neither a limit nor a transition, but an opening: with it, and in it, begins the great metamorphosis which brings us to unity: life and death are the two faces of the same reality. Human existence, says Rilke in a letter to a friend, "lives in these two limitless kingdoms" (death and life) "and takes endless nourishment from them . . . there is neither a before nor a beyond, but only the great unity, home of the beings who surpass us, the Angels . . . "[4] To reach the angelic state – or at least to catch a glimpse of it – is the destiny of all men and particularly of poets. Villaurrutia's vision of death could not be further from this; his death is closed, not open: a death that locks us in as it closes. Never could he have written – nor, perhaps, would he have wanted to write – these lines from the first elegy:

> Angels (they say) don't know whether it is the living
> they are moving among or the dead. The eternal torrent
> whirls all ages along in it, through both realms
> forever, and their voices are drowned out in its tremendous roar.[5]

In the same conversation with José Luis Martínez, Xavier mentions Heidegger and calls him "my philosopher." (Just as ingenuously, Heidegger declared, on reading the *Duino Elegies,* that Rilke was his poet.) We know that Villaurrutia came to Heidegger very late, when most of the poems of *Nostalgia for Death* had already been written. He himself made it clear that his encounter with Heidegger was more a confirmation than a revelation. It is worth recalling that Heidegger's vogue in the Spanish-speaking world began shortly before the Second World War. His influence in France, outside of an extremely limited sphere,

---

[4] Letter to W. von Hulewicz, cited by J.F. Angelloz in the study preceding his annotated introduction to the *Duino Elegies* and the *Sonnets to Orpheus* (Paris, 1943).
[5] Trans. Stephen Mitchell, in Mitchell, ed. *The Selected Poetry of Rainer Maria Rilke.*

began later. It should be added that even in Spain, permeated with German philosophy as it was during the years before the War, there was no more than a somewhat vague notion of Heidegger's thought. The only essay of his that had been translated into Spanish was, if I'm not mistaken, the famous text on nothingness, translated by Zubiri and published in the magazine *Cruz y Raya* [That's It]. The German philosopher first rose to dominance in 1937, the year of Antonio Machado's article, in *Hora de España* [Spanish Hour], on the vision of death in Heidegger's philosophy. The period of the Second World War saw the apogee of his influence in Hispanic America. This was brought about by various, mainly Spanish, philosophy teachers, particularly José Gaos. Mexico City and Buenos Aires were the two centers from which Heidegger's thought emanated.

The Contemporáneos – with the exception of Ramos – had only a tangential knowledge of phenomenology and existentialism. I don't mean that they were ignorant of Husserl or Heidegger: all of them were assiduous readers of *Revista de Occidente* [Review of the West] and its publications. But their relationship to phenomenology was rather distant and, above all, late. Their readings in phenomenology were not formative, like the readings of their youth. Though Cuesta wrote a piece on Scheler and the names of Husserl and Heidegger appear once or twice in his articles, the writers he truly admired were Valéry, Benda, and Gaston Bachelard (he was, in 1939, the first person to tell me about Bachelard). He was also a lifelong reader of Nietzsche, no doubt through the influence of Gide, who was among those who introduced his work in France. This is another of the traits that distinguish my generation from that of the Contemporáneos; our education included certain ideas that had barely touched them: Marxism, and phenomenology and Heideggerian thought, which we learned from the Spanish intellectuals who took refuge in Mexico and from their translations,

Towards 1930, the subject of death appears in Mexican literature. It then disappears, one more victim of the vast butchery of World War II. I don't mean to say that writers of other generations didn't mention the subject. I hardly need remind anyone that López Velarde, the Contemporáneos' immediate predecessor, wrote poems which revolve almost exclusively around the axis of love and death. But the Mexican writers of the thirties were under a kind of enthrallment, to the point that the period's three best books of poetry were titled *Muerte sin fin* [Death without End] (Gorostiza), *Nostalgia for Death* (Villaurrutia) and *Muerte de cielo azul* [Death of the Blue Sky] (Montellano). The almost simultaneous appearance of these three books is revealing, but what does it reveal? An obsession? An epidemic of melancholy? A style, an intellectual contagion? The historians of Mexican culture have not pondered this phenomenon. Why the sudden appearance of death in the consciousness, sensibility, and imagination of a group of Mexican poets?

Love and death, twins and adversaries, have been subject matter for poets since the origin of civilization. And even before that: one of the purest and most intense poems I know of is a pygmy funeral chant. But though the image of death has accompanied man from the beginning, periodically it becomes an obsessive preoccupation. Some eras are in love with death, others manage to exorcise it. In the consciousness of humanity, death appears and disappears with a certain cyclical regularity. Moreover, our idea of death changes over time and from society to society; there are as many visions of death as there are civilizations. Like all of mankind's other ideas and images, death is subject to change and renewal. It moves off of the intellectual horizon of a given period, then, after a time, returns. Each time it returns, it is different: renewal is change. Great changes – the death and birth of civilizations – manifest themselves through the emergence of an image of death. Each civilization has its own. The originality of Judeo-Christianity lay in its rupture of the cyclical time of paganism and its introduction of a new time, with a beginning and an end. The invention of Christian time would not have been possible without the appearance of a new image of death. For pagans, death was the end of individual existence, an episode in the circular, cosmic rebirth and redeath; for Christians, it was the doorway into another reality and another time. Christianity gave everyone his own death and made this death the key to eternity. Death ceased to be an end and became a beginning. What made Christianity radically different from paganism was its way of dying, its way of living death. And, likewise, all the oppositions between Christianity and Buddhism can be condensed into two images of death, the death of Christ and the death of the Buddha. The first dies at the age of thirty-three, nailed to a cross; the second dies at the age of eighty, stretched out under a sal tree, at the outskirts of a country estate, preaching to his disciples.

The double rhythm of renewal and change reveals itself within every civilization. In a famous book that has lost none of its original interest, Huizinga showed how the vision of death, allied with the vision of the carnival, gripped European consciousness at the end of the Middle Ages. The Burgundian death, lean and luxurious, returned during the Baroque period. It was the death of Charles le Téméraire and Villon, and it was something else: a sensual, worm-eaten, rational death alternatingly illuminated and obscured by the vainglorious fires of Donne and Quevedo. With Romanticism, death reigned supreme once more, but it was no longer the crowned, ermine-caped skeleton of the fifteenth century, or the seventeenth century's libertine *conceptista:* it was an inspired and prophetic shadow, speaking in dreams and indistinguishable from the night. Romanticism's death is feminine: woman and mother, universal vagina and dark, rich soil where cadavers rot and the terrible vegetations of the unconscious germinate. In the first third of the twentieth century, as a reaction, doubtless, to the positivist optimism of the second half of the nineteenth century, death presents itself anew. It is at once a romantic death and a death that laughs at Romanticism, and it is closely tied to the sensual arabesques of Art Nouveau and to the deliria of Dada and Surrealism. It is impossible to understand Dada without remembering that it was, initially and ultimately, the vertigo of confronting death. Dadaism is the moment when European aesthetic consciousness experiences the attraction of the void. In a Dada lecture given in Germany in 1922 – one of his last Dadaist texts and one of his best – Tristan Tzara explicitly associates Dada's nihilism with Buddhism. Surrealism transformed this vertigo into a fascination with the duality of existence: sleep and wakefulness, death and life. The emblem of this reality is the female fissure, adored and fearsome. In woman and in her sexual organ before and beyond are united... After the war the image of death faded from Western consciousness while its public reality grew to be omnipresent. In the wake of the atomic bomb and the concentration camps of Hitler and Stalin, it was difficult to feel a "nostalgia for death." Now, in the last few years, death has returned, but it is no longer philosophical or poetic; though men continue to kill each other as they always have, contemporary death is the reasonable muse of biologists, psychologists, and historians.

During the first third of the century, throughout most of the world and especially in Spain and Latin America, Dada, Surrealism and their ramifications represented the romantic aspect of the universal preoccupation with death. The opposite aspect was represented by the poetry written in English, though it was no less gripped by a consciousness of the fragility of men and their works. I am thinking especially of Eliot and of poems like *Ash Wednesday*. The center of this vast meditation on death was Germany, and its most notable figures were Rilke and Heidegger. The thought and poetry of our language were not insensible to so many stimuli. Perplexed by signs that seemed to predict its decline, terrified by the spectre – soon to become a reality – of a world war, the West turned its fascinated gaze towards the enigma we call dying: how could Spaniards and Hispanic Americans have failed to feel the same vertigo? Three centuries of prostration, defeat, and bloody convulsions had prepared them to participate in the meditation on their own cadaver to which European consciousness summoned them. It was only natural that Latin Americans contribute their poems and novels to this meditation. Our peoples, as I have tried to demonstrate elsewhere, are an extreme of the West. The other extreme is the Anglo-American world. Like all extremes, Latin America is eccentric, and this is particularly true of Brazil, Mexico, Peru, Bolivia and Guatemala. We are, moreover, a humiliated and ravaged continent. But no matter: without us, the modern literature of the West would be the poorer.

In the work of almost all the Spanish and Spanish-American poets of this period the subject of death appears. There are only a handful of exceptions: Jorge Guillén, Pellicer, and some others. But the poetry on this subject that was written in Spain and Latin America did not have the obsessive character that it had in Mexico. In the poetry of Gorostiza and Villaurrutia, death occupied the place that was occupied by eroticism and rebellion in Cernuda's work, and by time and identity in Borges's. In the work of other poets of the period – Neruda, García Lorca, Vicente Aleixandre – death is a magnetic center, indistinguishable from sexual passion, as in the title of a book by Aleixandre: *La destrucción o el amor* [Destruction or Love]. The disjunctive conjunction suggests, in this case, an equivalence: love is like destruction. In Borges's work, death appears a little earlier than among the Mexicans, but his death is neither private like Villaurrutia's nor the death of the universe, as in Gorostiza. For Villaurrutia, death was an experience lived from within his life – or, as they said then, a *vivencia,* a personal experience; for Borges, it is an example, an occasion for reflections and sententious epitaphs. Death in his poems is not his own death, but someone else's: a fellow citizen's. Not by chance is one of Borges's collections of poetry called *Muertes de Buenos Aires* [Deaths in Buenos Aires]. The plural is significant: death is others and because of that it is, as in the Stoics and Quevedo, a warning and the expectation of a punishment. Urban deaths: *caudillos,* heroes, low-lifes, and nameless corpses. Dead people on whose tombs Borges – sceptic and moralist who contradicts himself in order to be faithful to himself: he does not believe in the I, but he does believe in its death – writes his slow, somber lines. Lines that are also those of a lyric poet, a murmur of syllables like "the utterance of birds that allude, without knowing it, to death." Except that Borges *does* know.

The attitude of Villaurrutia and his friends is unintelligible if the intellectual and spiritual climate of the era in which they lived is not taken into account. All of them were keenly aware of being part of the West, and all of their cultural activity can be defined as an attempt to recuperate and reactivate European values. Not for nothing did they publish a magazine called *Contemporáneos.* None of them was an indigenist, except – very timidly – Montellano and, at the end of his life, Novo. I have already noted that their nationalism was a universalism and that for them, being Mexican meant reinserting themselves into the European tradition. According to Cuesta, the country's independence and the liberal reform of 1857 had aimed at separating us from the Spanish tradition (a dead Europe) in order to insert us into the republican and liberal tradition (a living Europe). For this reason, the true Mexican tradition, contrary to what the Romantics and the *modernistas* thought, was classicist in literature and, contrary to what the conservatives said, radical and republican in politics. (Cuesta's radicalism was closer to Alain than to Marx.) But this rather abstract universalism was not enough to make the European preoccupation with death their own. An interior predisposition was also necessary. I referred above to Villaurrutia's *melancholy,* in Nerval's sense of the word. Gorostiza and Cuesta also suffered from melancholia and acedia. Finally, apart from the personal inclinations and temperament of each one of them, the characteristic of the group I alluded to in the first part of this essay must be considered: its scepticism.

With the exception of Carlos Pellicer – different in this respect as in so many others – none of them adhered to the Catholic faith. Although Gilberto Owen professed at times to be a Catholic, his Catholicism, like Villaurrutia's, was paradoxical, more magical than religious, more exorcism than prayer. The ideas and beliefs of the Contemporáneos are not easily defined. They are more distinguished for their questions than for their affirmations or negations. Their scepticism made them abandon the traditional Mexican religion without opening the doors to any other system of belief. It would be useless to scan their work for traces of the "other religion" that in diverse forms – Kabbalah, alchemy, Analogist thought – has fascinated the poetic consciousness of the West since the Neoplatonic hermeticism of the Renaissance. This tradition, which is born in the Florence of Ficino and Pico de la Mirandola, infects Bruno and Campanella, influences the Elizabethan poets and those of the *Pléiade,* seduces Goethe and the German Romantics, reaches our century through the work of the French Symbolists and leaves its mark on Darío, Yeats, Pessoa, the Surrealists – this tradition was not theirs. The Contemporáneos lived in a zone of shifting sands: neither Eliot's Christianity nor Breton's "occultism" nor the materialism tinged with animism of Neruda. There comes a moment when a consistent scepticism makes the critic retreat from doubt. After this autocriticism, the sceptic – unless he resigns himself to silence – believes again, but not in the same things he believed in before, or in the same way. His beliefs do not aspire to justification through reason: they are content with their own authenticity. But the scepticism of the Contemporáneos was not radical and for that reason could not result in affirmations or negations, or in a pyrrhonic silence. Their scepticism was a vital doubt, not an intellectual method. It was not a philosophy but a belief that was, at the same time, a non-belief.

The Contemporáneos were faithful to reason and this often kept them from going astray. However, they were faithful to reason not for what it affirms but for what it negates. Their rationalism, if we can give their intelligent doubt that name, was an instrument for deconstructing systems, not for affirming anything. They reacted to the geometries of reason with the same indifference they had shown toward the mysteries of religion and magic. This was why they had so little feeling for the revolutionary utopias of our century. Naturally, this attitude cannot be explained on purely intellectual and philosophical grounds. The social and political circumstances of their childhood and youth, as I pointed out earlier in this essay, were in large measure responsible for determining their generation's disposition. In order to be understood, their scepticism must be seen in the context of the world in which they happened to live. They were "contemporaries" of Picasso and Eliot, but also of the great revolutionary disillusionment of Mexico. As early as 1930, it was already apparent that the history of Mexico was leading to a wall. A wall we are still unable to scale or to breach. Scepticism has a therapeutic social value: it immunizes us against affirmations and negations that are categorical and exclusive. It can thus preserve our liberty, since a tyrant or a slave is hidden in any man who affirms or negates without ever doubting. But the Contemporáneos, for the reasons I have given, could not have any faith in the social value of their doubt and so did not take their healthy scepticism into the fields of morality and politics. Reduced to solitude, they condemned themselves to self-analysis, and in the process of self-criticism and self-knowledge, the most lucid and rigorous of them – Gorostiza, Cuesta, Villaurrutia – had, inescapably, to meet with death.

Death is almost always associated with eroticism. Variations on this theme are innumerable and can be found in every historical period. In Gorostiza's great poem, sexuality occupies a limited space; his vision of love is sarcastic: the phallic flute and its "salacious serenade." Though Villaurrutia's erotic world is more intense, it is uninhabited: there are only shadows, echoes, reflections. Bodies are statues; flesh is stone or plaster; mouths are wounds. Unlike the death of Donne or Baudelaire, Villaurrutia's death is neither lascivious nor libertine. To find the union of sexuality and death in Mexican literature one must look to López Velarde or to the poets of my generation; one must look, above all, to the novels and fictions of Juan García Ponce and Salvador Elizondo. Eroticism is not a distinctive feature of the Contemporáneos' work. In Pellicer, there is a vision of the body, a sculptural sensuality, but not a true eroticism. Novo is the exception to this. Unfortunately, his eroticism, except in a few electric moments, generally verges on the scatological or the sentimental. Tears and excrement. None of the erotic poets of that generation – Neruda, Lorca, Pedro Salinas, Cernuda, Aleixandre – were Mexican.

In his prose work Villaurrutia occasionally alludes to Mexico as "the country of death." Nevertheless, neither his poetry nor Gorostiza's makes the least concession to local color. The painting of this period abounds with skulls, skeletons, the candles and yellow flowers of wakes, coffins, crosses, and processions, all the pomp of Mexican death, lyrically celebrated at moments, depicted with sarcasm and black humor at others, or protested – proletarian death covered with red banners. But the poetry of Villaurrutia and Gorostiza seems to have been written not only in some other country, but in a place beyond geography and history, beyond myth and legend, a nowhere that "occupies no place in space," in which time has stopped. And here, once again, Ortiz de Montellano stands out in contrast. He is a poet to whom more attention should be paid, not so much for what he succeeded in doing as for what he tried to do. Because of the prophetic value he attributed to sleep, Ortiz de Montellano was closer to the true Romanticism and the true Surrealism. In certain of his poems death appears in the guise of a Mexican funeral:

> A hut with three toy figures,
> arches of flowers,
> the offering to the corpse:
> four yellow veils
> of sempasóchil flowers.[6]

In the poetry of Gorostiza and Villaurrutia the burial rituals of the Mexican people do not appear, nor do those of the pre-Columbian civilization; the splendors with which the poetry of the Baroque period

[6] *Jacal de tres juguetes,*
arcos de flores,
la ofrenda del cadáver:
cuatro amarillas velas
de sempasóchil.

enveloped death are absent as well. For the Aztecs, death was a moment in the cosmic movement, a conception which is not far from Gorostiza's circular death. Aztec poetry contains images and intuitions that are close to the idea of "one's own death" which so preoccupied Villaurrutia. But neither poet makes the slightest allusion to the pre-Columbian world. Both were admirably well-acquainted with the poetry of the Baroque period and traces of Góngora are as numerous in *Death without End* as those of Quevedo, Calderón and Sor Juana are in *Nostalgia for Death*. But these influences have undergone a curious operation, as if they had passed through a sort of vacuum chamber, so that the images and metaphors, without losing any of their power or their consistency, have become immaterial: crystals in Gorostiza's poetry, reflections in Villaurrutia's. Gorostiza's death is incarnated in all forms and ends up having no form whatsoever. It is as untouchable as an idea, as invisible as a transparency. Villaurrutia's death is more personal, more intimate, but no less intangible. Borges's dead are bodies, there, stretched out in front of us in the wake's fantastic light. Or they are the dead of urban cemeteries: a gravestone or a pile of bricks and stones protects them from our gaze, not a skein of concepts. They are a reality, incomprehensible, perhaps, but real. Villaurrutia's death is "the companion you speak to when you are alone," the voice without a body, the voice that does not speak words, the voice that says nothing. Villaurrutia had an extraordinary visual sensibility and almost all of his poems are paintings, but they are uninhabited paintings: the central figure, death or love, is not there. Or rather: it is an invisible presence, the wind moving the curtains, the shadow drowning in the mirror.

Death fulfills itself in the ritual of burial: think of all the great burials of Western painting and literature, from El Greco to Courbet, from Mark Anthony's funeral oration over Caesar's corpse, in Shakespeare, to the verses Hugo composed for Gautier's burial. I have mentioned Borges's wakes, and I should add García Lorca's *Lament for Ignacio Sánchez Mejías*. In Mexico, a country where until very recently burial was a public art, a poetry of death emerged that deliberately disdained not only all of the visual and sensual elements of that art but also any form of anecdote or affective particularity. In Villaurrutia's death—and the same can be said of Gorostiza's—there is no *earth*, in any sense of the word. The opposition between death and life is not expressed, in

Villaurrutia's work, through the funerary ritual of burial, but as an opposition between sleep and wakefulness. In one of his *Epitaphs* (dedicated to his own death or to Jorge Cuesta's?) he says that "to wake is to die." This paradox illuminates his vision of death and his poetry. Sleeping was always "the image of death" but Villaurrutia inverts the terms of the ancient metaphor: sleeping is the image of life and we will die if we awaken. Death is life. Xavier wanted to suggest, in this way, that in the state of wakefulness, if we are lucid, we live our own death. The content of our life is our death. We are inhabited by it. Inhabited or uninhabited? It is all the same: death is a vacant presence, a present absence. For Villaurrutia, the emblem of death is not burial: death is an exile. An exile that is simultaneously a return: our true homeland is death and that is why we feel a nostalgia for it. Though death is the great mother, it is neither vagina nor tomb but an unlimited and vacant space. Like every poet, Villaurrutia transmuted the circumstances of his life and his world: the theme of interior exile, common to all those of his generation, fallen into a hostile environment where they were always treated as strangers, became a vision of death as homeland:

> To go back to the distant country,
> to go back to the forgotten country,
> secretly deformed
> by exile in this land.

THE EDITION of Xavier Villaurrutia's *Complete Works* published in 1966 by the Fondo de Cultura Económica is more than a thousand pages long. Nonetheless, for the majority of his readers, Villaurrutia is the author of some fifteen or twenty poems. Is this meager? To me it seems like a great deal. Because of these poems, we remember the plays and we reread the critical essays: we want to find in them, if not the secret of his poetry, at least the secret of the fascination that it holds for us. These twenty-odd poems count among the best in our language and of his time. Does the place that Villaurrutia occupies in Mexico and Latin America correspond to this excellence? The answer, frankly, is no. Villaurrutia has no reputation in Europe and his poetry is seldom read. The reason is not difficult to see. His poetry is a solitary poetry, a poetry for those who are solitary; it does not seek the complicity of the passions that tyrannize our spirits today: politics, patriotism, ideologies. No church, no party, no State can gain anything from propagating poems whose subjects – or, rather, obsessions – are sleep, solitude, insomnia, sterility, death. Even eroticism, the great fetish of our frigid, cruel century, appears in his poems as a secret passion whose most visible attributes are rage, drought, impotence, and aridity. There is nothing in this poetry to attract readers who, like the majority of our contemporaries, reduce all of life, even instinctive and sexual life, to ideological categories. Villaurrutia's poetry is not antisocial but asocial.

The Mexican government, that great embalmer and petrifier of celebrities, has displayed a sovereign indifference to the work and the memory of Villaurrutia. Perhaps it's better this way: he has been spared the grotesque statue and the alley bearing his name. (In Mexico, the wide avenues and the public squares belong, by self-proclaimed right, or, I was about to say, by *droit du seigneur,* to the ex-presidents and the powerful. The streets of our cities have been branded, like so many cattle, with names that are frequently infamous.) Neither has Mexican public opinion – I mean the intellectuals and the pedants – demonstrated much love for Villaurrutia's poetry. But his case is not exceptional: the literate and semi-literate among us gazed with similar disdain on Tablada, Pellicer, Gorostiza, Reyes, González Martínez, and even López Velarde. Villaurrutia's glory is secret, like his poetry. I don't regret this and neither would he. He asked for nothing more than the fervent admiration of a few. In modern times poetry is not, nor can it be, more than an underground cult, a ceremony in the catacomb.

Villaurrutia was always preoccupied by the opposition between Classicism and Romanticism. These terms did not have an exclusively historical and stylistic meaning for him; their meaning was vital and personal. The opposition between them was his conflict, his drama. There are poets gripped by unity, as if reality and language itself were emanations of the Plotinian One, poets of being, not dispersed into multiplicity but resolved into essence. Jorge Guillén is such a poet. There are other poets for whom the world and language are waves of a fecund and confused substance, anterior to unity, a genetic, indistinct, rhythmical substance. Pablo Neruda is such a poet. Xavier Villaurrutia's poetry is defined neither by a unity of essence nor by a plural substance, but by its duality. His poetry originates in a consciousness of duality, and is an attempt to resolve that duality into a unity, a unity that will not destroy the duality but will, on the contrary, preserve it, and in it preserve itself. For Xavier, one was always two.

The opposition between Classic and Romantic is one of the forms taken by the contradiction that inhabited him. It isn't hard to find other oppositions in every one of his poems: solitude/companionship, silence/sound, sleep/wakefulness, time/eternity, fire/ice, plenitude/void, nothing/all . . . Villaurrutia did not attempt, in his poems, the transmutation of this into that – flame into ice, void into plenitude – but the perception and expression of the moment of transition between opposites. The paradoxical instant in which the snow begins to darken but without yet becoming shadow. Borderline states in which we are present at a kind of universal doubling. In this doubling we witness not the coincidence of opposites, as Nicolás de Cusa would have it, but their coexistence. The word that defines this is the preposition *between*. In the vertiginous and provisional zone that opens up between two realities, in this *between* that is the bridge hanging over the void of language, in the sandy, sterile bank at the edge of the precipice – that is where the poetry of Villaurrutia places itself, takes root, and grows. A prodigious, transparent tree made of reflections, shadows, and echoes.

Between is not a space; it is what is between one space and another; neither is it time, but the moment that blinks between before and after. *Between* is neither here nor now. *Between* is neither body nor substance. Its kingdom is the phantasmal realm of antinomies and paradoxes. *Between* lasts as long as lightning. In its light, man can see himself as the arc that instantaneously unites this and that without truly uniting them and without being one or the other – or being both at once without being either. Man: the wakeful sleeper, the cold flame, the lump of shadow, the punctual eternity . . . This intermediary state, neither this nor that but between this and that, between rational and irrational, between night and day, wakefulness and sleep, life and death – what is it?

The intermediary state, in Villaurrutia's poetry, designates a moment of extreme attention in the center of an even more extreme abandon: to sleep with one's eyes open, to see with one's eyes closed. The intermediary state has another name: agony. It is also called doubt.

About what? About being but also about not being. The poet doubts, looks at himself in a mirror, perceives himself as a reflection, drowns himself in a flash of light. Doubt is agony: death and resurrection in a minute as long as the creation and destruction of all the worlds. The poet is a ghost and the echo of his cry as he pounds on the wall is a fist pounding a hollow breast, a blank page, a tarnished mirror that opens out onto a gallery of echoes. Not metaphors, but instantaneous visions of man *between* presences and absences. *Between:* the lacuna. The universal pause, the vacillation of things between what they are and what they will be . . .

Between is the universal fold. The doubling-over that reveals, when it is unfolded, not unity but duality, not essence but contradiction. The fold hides between its closed pages the two faces of being: the fold, as it reveals what it hides, hides what it reveals; the fold, as it opens its two wings, closes them; the fold says *No* each time it says *Yes;* the fold is its own duplicity: its double, its assassin, its complement. The fold is that which unites opposites without ever merging them, at equal distances from unity and plurality. In poetic topology, the geometric figure of the fold represents the *between* of language: the semantic monster that is neither this nor that, an oscillation identical to immobility, a frozen fluctuation. The fold, as it unfolds, is a leap that is stopped before it touches the ground—and as it refolds? The fold and *between* are two of the forms assumed by the unanswerable question. Villaurrutia's poetry folds itself into this question and unfolds between the oppositions that sustain it:

> Who can stake out the space, foretell the moment
> when the ice will overrun my body and envelop
> this unpulsing heart like a cold flame?

— Mexico, September 30, 1977.

ELIOT WEINBERGER'S essays are collected in *Works on Paper* and *Outside Stories,* and his transla-·tions include *Collected Poems of Octavio Paz* and Jorge Luis Borges's *Seven Nights.* He was the first recipient of the PEN/Kolovakos Award for lifetime achievement in the promotion of Latin American literature in the U.S.

ESTHER ALLEN is the translator of Blaise Cendrar's *Modernities and Other Writings* and has recently completed a study of nineteenth century travel writing between the Americas.